AF560608

DPH SPORTS SERIES

TENNIS

H. C. DUBEY

DISCOVERY PUBLISHING HOUSE
New Delhi-110002

Reprinted - 2019

First Published - 1999

ISBN: 978-81-7141-454-3

Tennis

Published by:

DISCOVERY PUBLISHING HOUSE PVT. LTD.

4383/4B, Ansari Road, Darya Ganj
New Delhi-110 002 (India)
Phone: +91-11-23279245, 23253475; 43596065
E-mail: discoverybooksindia@gmail.com
discoverypublishinghouse@gmail.com
web: www.discoverypublishinggroup.com

Printed at:
Infinity Imaging Systems
Delhi

PREFACE

The need of having a sports series felt because today's situation of the world is not conducive to peace, all round there is destruction, despair, conflict and war; war if not between two nations then within the country itself. In a world where there are some 820 million people unemployed or under-employed, and where 86 million people are born every year, it is not surprising that one out of every four individuals lives in absolute poverty. The *Discovery Publishing House* by Publishing this series seeks to get positive response as—to means by which sports can promote and propagate peace and international cooperation. Sportsmen form a large identifiable cadre. We visualises a situation where a conscious efforts is made all over the world to train the sportspersons to spread the message of peace and international cooperation. Instead of peace keeping efforts through arms and army, the sportspersons may be used as soldiers of peace in a subtle manner. The effort is to make the realize the contribution of sports as a factor for sustainable development, peace keeping and international cooperation.

In developing countries, sports development cooperation is still in the need of justification and steadfast arguments. Many people ask the question "why invest in sports in developing countries for which water supply, health service and agriculture projects are much better suited? An apt reply to this question may be "for many of the people of a developing country,

Sports is the only 'Sweaty' Leisure-time activity. Sports represents a moment of joy in the midst of hard poverty-stricken and dirty everyday life. Doing sports even makes one's work go more smoothly the next day.

This series will be useful to the sports promoters, organisers, coaches and other persons related or interested in sports.

Editor

CONTENTS

1

PRINCIPLES OF TENNIS

Tennis is a basically simple game which involves opposing players who stroke the ball back and forth over a net into the court. Play continues until one of the players hits the ball out of the court, into the net, or does not stoke the ball before it bounces twice. Play is started when one player (the server) stands behind the base line and to the right of the centre mark and puts the ball in play by tossing it in the air and striking it with his racket so that it lands in the right service court on the opposite side of the net. This player has then "served" the ball to his opponent. The opposing player (the receiver) must let the served ball bounce and then must hit it into his opponent's court, between the side lines, the base line, and the net. Balls are hit alternately until one of the players fails to return the ball into his opponent's court. After the service, balls can be played before they have bounced or on the first bounce. Points are scored according to the official United States Tennis Association (USTA) rules. After the first point is completed, the server moves to the left of the centre mark and serves into his opponent's left service court. Subsequently, he alternates service courts for every point. A designated number of points makes up a game; games make up a set, and sets, a match.

In doubles, two players on one side oppose two players on another side. The idea of the game, however, remains essentially the same as in singles. Players serve in turn in doubles, first a member of one team, then a member of the other team, and so on. However, players need not take turns hitting the ball after it is in play following a return of service.

As in sports there are basic fundamentals. In tennis these are a good grip and proper tennis form. The latter includes the swing and hitting the ball, footwork, and timing.

The fundamentals of lawn tennis are affected more perhaps by the player's grip of the racket than anything else that is within his control. His playing position, his swing, the twist the ball receives, all depend on the grip he has on his racket when he hits the ball. There has been controversy over the best methods of gripping the racket almost since the birth of the game. There have been three distinct schools, each of which has its merits, and beyond these a half dozen eccentric styles of holding the racket have earned more or less success. But while we find that certain methods of gripping have apparent advantages for certain strokes, they lose in other strokes as much or more than is gained. It is not practicable to change the hold for every stroke, so some set style must be adopted that gives the most advantage for all the strokes required.

A slight shifting, for instance, in the position of the hand gives a much better hold for the rolling backhand drive, but only for this stroke, and so it is available only for those players who use this stroke regularly. If this is adopted, then other strokes on the backhand side must be adapted to this hold or suffer in consequence.

There are three *major* different types of grips: the Eastern, the Continental, and the Western. The basic difference between the three is position of the palm of the hand. In the Western grip, the palm is under the handle; in the Continental, it is over it; while in the Eastern, the palm is behind the handle.

Eastern grip. This is the most popular grip today, being used by over 70 percent of American players. It is recommended for the novice by most experts. It is equally good for dealing with high, waist-high, or very low shots.

The Eastern grip is made by holding the racket at the throat with the left hand and extending it comfortably in front of you with the butt end of the handle toward your body. The face of the racket should be at right angles to the ground. Grasp the racket with the right hand so that the back knuckle of the thumb is directly on top of the racket, about an eighth of an inch to the left of centre. This means that the V or wishbone formed between the forefinger and the handle. The butt of the racket should rest easily on the heel of the hand. The thumb is wrapped around the racket and the fingers extended comfortably along the handle. The palm of the hand should be against the back plane of the handle. This grip is often described as "shaking hands with the racket." A lefthanded player should do the above procedure by holding the racket with the right hand and grasping it with the left. The backhand grip can be obtained from the Eastern forehand grip by shifting the hand to the left (counter clockwise) about one quarter of a turn. This should bring the back knuckle of the first finger directly on top of the racket. Now, the V between the thumb and forefinger will come just at the inner edge of the handle and your thumb will point diagonally across the handle. By having part of the thumb behind the racket, this grip gives added support and control to the stroke. The change from the forehand to the backhand is made by using the left hand to help guide the racket. This can be accomplished while you are in the anticipatory position or during the backswing.

Continental grip. For the Continental grip, the handle is rotated about an eighth of a turn (counter clockwise by righthanders, clockwise by left-handers) from the Eastern grip. Since the Continental grip is halfway between the Eastern forehand and backhand grips, it is good for either of these two basic groundstrokes without the necessity of shifting the hand grip. It also facilitates making short cross-court shots and, in addition, is excellent for dealing with low bounces. However, unless your wrist is very strong, you will find it difficult to control high-bounding balls.

The Continental grip is made by standing the racket on one edge and then simply picking it up from that position. In so doing, the palm of the hand is virtually on top of the racket and the thumb extends across the front of the handle. Many top Australian players use the Continental grip because of their emphasis on net play even in the beginning stages of learning. The no-change feature of the grip makes it especially suitable for the fast action required there, and doubtless grips into back-count play.

Western grip. This grip is very good for dealing with high shots and suitable for waist-high balls, but is difficult to use on very low shorts. In other words, it is not as good as all-around grip as the other two, and hence is the least used of the three.

The Western grip is obtained by laying the racket face down on the ground and then picking it up in the same manner as the Continental. This places the palm of the hand underneath the handle when the racket head is brought into a vertical or hitting position.

There is no general agreement as to precisely when the hand has left the range of the Eastern grip to become, let us say, a Continental or, if moved in thee other direction, a Western. This is simply a matter of semantics. Actually, some players, over the years, have used variations or combinations of these grips and some have even used unorthodox ones. For example, Pancho Segura—who had one of the best forehand drives—used an unorthodox two-handed grip. Likewise, John Bromwich, the Australian great, used both hands on the handle for the backhand at all. They shifted the racket from right hand to left and played forehands on either side. Such a style has a major disadvantage when it comes to rapid net play.

Whether you use an Eastern, a Continental, or a Western grip, there is only one way to hold the racket—with firm fingers. The racket is your weapon and it must move the ball; if you hold it loosely, the ball will twist the racket in your hand and you will have no control.

Many players, when trying to grip the racket firmly, will tighten up the whole arm. The arm itself should be relaxed. All strokes (with the exception of the moment of impact on serve and overhead) are hit with a bent arm. On ground-strokes, the arm wheels freely from shoulder and elbow on the backswing, and the arm is bent slightly on the hit. It becomes almost straight only on the follow-through. It becomes stiff only when one stretches wide for a ball almost out of reach. The arm is also bent on the volley, again the only exception being the side ball. Learning to keep the fingers firm and the arm relaxed is a prerequisite to good tennis. At first the arm will always stiffen. It is like learning to pat your stomach with your left hand and rub your head with a circular motion with your right hand; in the beginning both hands will perform the same motion, and it takes concentration to make them act out different motions simultaneously.

The wrist should be as firm as the fingers. Beginners and intermediates should practice hitting the ball with a wrist that is absolutely locked during the hit. If the wrist is loose, the ball moves the racket instead of the racket moving the ball. Wrist and arm are practically one straight line on the backhand groundstrokes and volley; wrist and arm form a 20-degree angle on forehand groundstroke and volley. The wrist snaps only on the service and overhead.

The player should be well past the intermediate stage before he ever tries to put wrist action into his groundstrokes. When he has learned to stroke the ball well with firm fingers, locked wrist, and relaxed arm, he can introduce "wrist" shots into his game. The "wrist" movements are necessary for slice, drop shots, chops, and the angle or touch game; if they are acquired too soon, the player may never learn a solid set of groundstrokes.

When wrist is introduced into a player's

repertoire, he is at a stage when he understands that the wrist moves the ball, not the ball the wrist. To hit groundstrokes with such an action, the wrist must be strong as iron and the timing must be perfect. It is not a shot for a beginner.

To rest the hand from the fatigue of constant tight tripping, relax the grip between the strokes, and if necessary help to carry the weight by resting the neck of the racket in the left hand between shots.

Always grip the racket by the very end; never shorten the grip. This is the hardest thing to impress on the beginner's mind, because he finds it more difficult to swing the racket at first with the full length of the handle, and he is very reluctant to do this, when the shorter grip gives him a quicker control and permits him to hit the ball with a jerky half swing. At first the beginner swings his racket only a foot or two in striking, making more of a push than a blow of his stroke, and this lets him delay striking until the last second, and the stroke seems easier to be made in this way. But the error of this method is that it depends on the strength of the player's arm for success, and this is the first great fallacy by which the novice is led into bad habits of play. The arm's strength has little to do with the good tennis stroke; it depends almost entirely on the momentum of the racket, and at the moment of impact little or no strength is exerted by the arm.

As in golf, the player "presses" as soon as be uses his muscles too much. The racket and the golf club really do the work required, and it is only necessary for the player to start them in the right direction, and increase their momentum and speed by the swing of the body and arm until they reach the maximum when the ball is hit. He need only guide the racket or club, rather than push it along.

The length of the racket is increased by every inch of the handle that is extended beyond the gripping hand, so that its leverage and the power of its swing under momentum increase fast with this extension. As it is difficult to shift the grip after first habits are formed, it is doubly important to begin with the long grip, even though it seems more difficult at first.

The reluctance of most beginners to grip the handle by the extreme end comes from the difficulty of making a successful stroke with only a half swing and a long grip. The novice hesitates to make a full swing because he cannot calculate at first so far ahead where the ball is going to bound and how high and how deep it will jump up in front of him. He fears to draw his racket far back to make the stroke because he expects to make only a half swing.

The leather "button," or binding at the end of the handle helps to prevent the racket from slipping from the hand, and also warns the player, without his needing to look down, when his hand has reached the end of the handle. This leather end should rest against the fleshy part of the hand at the base of the thumb, and, if the full-length grip is cultivated, it will rest very comfortably there while in play.

The size of the handle is an important point. There is a tendency to have it too large. It should be of such diameter that it fills the hand but allows the fingers to work. If it is too large this is impossible. The smaller the handle the quicker is the work of hand and fingers. On the other hand, there is the principle that the handle should be large enough to act as a strut in the hand, and so keep the wrist firm. The best size is that which makes the thumb and middle finger overlap to the extent of about an inch, not less in any case, but very little more Good form in any sport is one of those elusive qualities that are hard to describe, and often harder to adopt. Briefly defined, good form, so far as it applies to lawn tennis, may be said to be the manner and method of playing which will produce in the hands of the average man the greatest percentage of success. It is that method of using the body, the arms, and the lets which gives the greatest freedom and the best ability to make successful strokes.

There have been many players and some experts who have won high honours despite bad form, and too often have these men been followed as models simply because it was though that their success vindicated their methods. But this is an empty fallacy, for such a player may have certain mental or physical qualities that are entirely foreign to the average player. Abnormal length of arms or legs may affect his manner of swinging his racket or the position he assumes during play. The same methods adopted by a player of a different mold would not give the same results.

Three of the elements of good tennis form are sound strokes, perfect balance, and proper timing. A well-founded stroke gives the player the equipment to deal with the ball, good balance enables the player to hit with the full force of his weight and regain his ready position immediately thereafter, and fine timing allows the player to meet the ball at the right moment. There are other factors in the good player's repertoire—anticipation, footwork, stamina, a cool head, the will to win, strategy, and so on—but these are the refinements of match play and are developed as the player moves to higher levels. First the player must acquire good strokes, good balance, and good timing. The swing and hitting the ball. Whether you make a forehand or backhand, a lift or slice stroke, the general principles involved are much the same, and a thorough study of these will help.

Three distinct actions must be kept in mind, although they frequently all run into one with such rapidity that it is hard to separate them. First we have the backswing in preparation for the stroke; then the act of hitting the ball, and finally the follow-through. To hit the ball properly, the eyes should be kept on the ball until it is hit, and in calling attention to this, it should be pointed out that "keeping the eye on the ball" means actually focusing the eyes on the ball as it approaches. A player should have a sense of bringing the focus in as the ball comes toward him. By so doing, the inside muscles of the eyes will become tired sooner, but the effort will be worthwhile. Most beginning players fail to do this and too often look through the ball. This means that as the ball leaves the opponent's racket the eyes are fixed on it but as it comes toward the player he does not bring the focus in with the advance of the ball. Most persons can unconsciously gauge with great accuracy their distance from an object on which eyes are properly focused. Nothing will help you to hit with the centre of the racket, the shot is generally flubbed, or at least, is ineffective. Therefore, all through the stroke, be careful to keep your head down and your eye on the ball.

During play there are times when it is necessary to see where an opponents is, and to glance at the court and its boundary lines. Expert players also use a special finesse in the higher are of expert play, in which they look away from the ball just before they hit it, in order to direct a placed shot more accurately. But this kind of technique is not for beginners, and should be put aside entirely until the player is well on the road to expert skill.

Only by watching the ball constantly will it be possible to calculate the angle of its flight, the distance it will travel before striking, and how high and bow far it will bound before you must hit it. The ball in any sharp light offers a fine mark, and the eye can be focused on it no matter how fat it may fly through the air. Whether it is coming or going, so long as the play continues, it must be followed constantly if one is to play well.

The anticipatory, or readiness, position should be somewhat crouching, with bent knees, shoulders thrown well forward, and the weight carried up on the toes. Ready to spring in any direction on the instant, the player in this position is wonderfully able to reach the return that may be placed in some other part of the court. He should always be ready to move quickly, and even when the ball comes directly toward him, he should jump forward in striking. The greatest power in making any stroke comes from leaning to meet the ball, which brings all the player's weight into the blow.

As soon as your opponent hits the ball you should as quickly as possible determine the direction of the ball, then determine whether you are going to receive it on the forehand or backhand. Immediately upon making this decision you should carry the racket back into position for the stroke, whether on forehand or backhand. In the event of an overhead smash, it is well to get the racket back and up in position well ahead of time.

The reasons for this precaution are very sound, as well as obvious. If the racket is in position to make the stroke when the ball reaches you, can go through with the stroke easily, without hurrying, without jerking, and the stroke is more than likely to be well timed and sound. If you await the arrival of the ball before getting the racket in position, you must take the backswing and return to the point of contact with the ball so quickly that accuracy is very difficult. If you get your racket back as soon as your opponent hits the ball, you are more than likely to be able to handle the position of your feet. In running to receive the ball, at the same time get the racket back, or up in case of a smash, in position to make the stroke.

A good test to see if you are getting the racket back early enough in anticipation of the stroke and getting it back properly is to note whether you have started for position on balls which your opponent has hit toward your court, but which have been stopped by the net. If you have started toward the correct position before the ball hits the net, you will know that you are anticipating reasonably well. If you have not started before the ball is netted, you will know that your anticipation is bad.

As soon as you know the ball is coming to your forehand or your backhand, swing your shoulders to the right or to the left, as the case may be, so that the shoulders are at right angle to the net. You should be able to tell whether the ball is going to be on the forehand or the backhand before the ball in flight is on your side of the net. If you swing your shoulders in time your feet will have the tendency to move more easily and to cooperate more smoothly so you may be in correct position for a proper stroke. Taking advantage of all the time available for getting into proper position assures you ample time to make your shot unhurried. Shots made in a great hurry cannot consistently be good shots.

A full and free backswing is most essential. It is not necessary, as in golf, to wrap your arm and racket around your neck in order to get the full impetus necessary for a hard drive, but a stroke that starts only a foot or two back of the point of impact with the ball is unlikely to have any great power. In fact, the power of a tennis stroke depends almost entirely on the momentum of the racket, and this is gained largely by the swing that adds the weight of the body to the force. Little if any muscle is required to make a good stroke. The well-timed swing of the arm and racket, accelerated by body swing, and the all-important "follow-through" are what do the work. Not only is the swing of the body before the ball is hit needed to produce a good stroke, but it should be carried far beyond that point, following the ball long after it has left the racket. This follow-through, so much talked of in golf, is equally important in tennis, and the fastest strokes of expert players are the result of perfect timing to secure the maximum momentum in the racket, added to a full follow-through of the body weight.

A good player starts his windup when he runs. He does not wait until he gets to the ball. If he had to run wide on his forehand, he starts his semicircular (or straight-back_ backswing immediately. By the time he has reached the ball, the racket has begun its forward motion. The only time a player can start his backswing after his feet are planed for the shot is against a soft hitter. The more pace the opponent has on his ball, the sooner the windup must begin. Beginners invariably start their backswing after the ball has cleared the net; advanced players start as soon as the ball leaves the opponent's racket. Players in the intermediate category frequently show a tendency to be late either on forehand windup, backhand windup, or on the backswing when running for a short ball or drop shot.

A top player always looks ready because he starts his windup in plenty of time; a lesser player always looks rushed because he waits too long to begin the stroke.

At the back of its preliminary swing the racket must pause anyway and lose its momentum before starting forward, so that it can be checked for a slightly longer period if necessary, if you should unintentionally swing too early for the stroke. It is far better to err on this side than on the other, so it is a safe rule to keep swinging back earlier until you find you must noticeably check the racket before starting the forward swing for the stroke. This pause at the end of the backswing has an inclination to steady the stroke, but it can easily be exaggerated and it then has a tendency, particularly when marked, to expose the direction of the attack.

The total absence of any pause may result in hurrying the stroke too much, and the tendency to "snap" on the ball which follows this habit invariably results in a loss of control. If full time is not allowed and the forward swing is hurried, the slightest deviation of the ball from the expected flight will result in a bad stroke, as there is no time left to correct the swing to meet this shift.

At the end of the reach backward, you will notice that the arm swings naturally either upward or sidewise behind you. By all means, select the upward motion. This keeps the racket in the direct line of flight and avoids the side motion that is so apt to throw off the accuracy of the stroke as well as the body's poise during the forward stroke. You should also increase somewhat the arc of this circle in the backswing by turning slightly with the shoulders so that you have the longest reach possible without getting out of position for a free stroke. The shoulders at the end of the backswing should be parallel with the feet and the line of flight of the ball. The weight of the body, too, should be shifted full on the back foot and when making a strong stroke, it should be swung back as far as possible to preserve the balance.

If you find that you run well on either side but that you make too many errors when running in for short balls or drops shots, the fault may lie in the fact that you are not ready. Start your windup as you run forward. The backswing is not only completed by the racket should actually be moving forward when you reach the ball. Errors are corrected by exaggerations in the other direction. If you have been late on your windup, get your racket back the moment the ball leaves the opponent's racket, even if it makes you too early for the ball.

When the time is right to begin the forward swing, that is, to make the stroke, the body turns on the hips, the right shoulder comes forward, followed by the upper arm, and then the forearm; and finally just before the ball is hit, the wrist adds the snap of a whiplash to the blow and the full weight of the body shifts quickly forward from the backward to the forward foot, so that at the moment of impact all possible energy is concentrated in the blow.

Now comes the greatest difficulty that is found in the play of most players. They are inclined to stop here. After hitting the ball, they feel that is as far as they can control it, and they make no effort to follow through, recovering the balance as quickly as possible in the most convenient way. But this is all wrong. Just as in golf, the follow-through is most important. While it is true that after the ball has once left the racket, it is impossible to further affect its movements, the after swing of the player does affect the whole stroke most materially. It is impossible to make a true stroke without it, since any effort to cut short the swing infallibly affects the stroke itself and draws the racket away from its work before its maximum power has been exerted.

The racket should not only follow the ball itself just as far as you can normally reach, but you should also bend the whole body as far as the balance will allow to lengthen the swing of the arm. The entire body should be turned on the hips, the bent knees allowing it to move forward with the stroke and extend the swing of the racket. At the end of this following swing, the body should turn still further around, the shoulders pulling in, the arm and the wrist bending to allow the racket's impetus to be checked with a short swing like the *moulinet* of the swordsman.

For the most exaggerated groundstrokes, the weight of the body is thrown so violently forward in the follow-through that the balance is frequently checked by carrying the back foot forward to a further advanced position. Indeed this style is not at all uncommon, and where well practised it almost invariably increases the body swing, the follow-through, and the power of the stroke. It is an excellent habit to allow the weight to draw the back foot forward to a new position, and the habit of taking this forward step in making the stroke will add greatly to the vigour of the attack.

The method should be used sparingly when the player is well forward in his court, for if the weight is thrown too far forward when in the volleying position, it is easy to lose the balance forward and become exposed to an overhead attack by a lob before the balance can be recovered.

Now, through all these three motions of the stroke, one cardinal rule should always be kept in mind. Every motion should be as far as possible in the direct line of the ball's flight; every motion that is off this line tends to lessen or check the power of the stroke and to lessen its accuracy. Side motion of any kind only weakens the swing.

It is not an uncommon fault among beginners to see the player bend his body backward away from the ball, particularly in making the forehand groundstroke. This only serves to detract from the body swing by checking the forward motion of the weight. Swinging the racket across the face of the ball to exaggerate the cut checks the forward force of the stroke and sometimes loses more in speed than it gains in the twist. The more directly every motion can be kept in line with the flight to intended for the ball, the more accurate will be the aim of the player and the more power there will be in the stroke. Side motions of the racket and arm almost invariably mean lost power and cause poor direction as well. The player who swings his racket across the path of the ball, rather than directly after it in the same plane, is generally wild in his returns and funds it difficult to control the ball as he should.

It is practically impossible to make a good stroke when the ball is played from close to the body. One should keep away from it in every direction. As it approaches, keep further back than you think necessary, and then jump forward to meet it, which gives the much-needed body weight in the stroke. Sidewise, also, never let the ball approach directly toward your body. Rather keep it off to one side and lean out to meet it, again using the balance of the body to add weight to the stroke. When a ball comes straight at you, step to one side or the other or your stroke will be ruined.

The elbow becomes bent and cramped when the ball gets in close to the player's body, and there is little or no power in a stroke made from such a position. If the ball bounds to the right or left of what was expected, the difference can be taken up by the bend of the elbow if well extended, but when cramped, all chance to correct the error in calculating the ball's flight is lost.

The idle arm should be used as a counterbalance. With it extended far out in the opposite direction from that carrying the racket, the balance can be preserved much better, and it also permits the player to lean farther out to meet the ball and to use his body weight in the stroke.

Watch a man run and you will see that whenever his right leg goes forward, his right arm swings back, and the same with the left. Without the arms swinging as counterbalances, it would not be possible for him to run nearly so fast, as the efforts of his legs would throw him off his balance with no help from the arm on the opposite side. It is the same thing in tennis, and the value of the idle arm as a counterbalance in fast play cannot be overestimated.

In all groundstrokes, where a full swing is called for, and in most others, the player should turn his side toward the net when he makes the stroke. This gives a free swing for the racket and brings the foot into line so that the weight can be shifted from one to the other during the stroke to increase the body swing that is so necessary for speed. In stepping into this position, the player moves forward with one foot or backward with the other, according to whether the next ball is coming short or deep into his court.

Except while making a few volleys at the net, it is best to loosen up the joints so that the swing of the racket is not jerky. A pliable wrist is a great help, and the "flick" of the racket just before the ball is hit, by which experts add so much to their speed, all comes from the wrist. The more the like a whiplash, the smoother and more powerful will be the stroke. The arm acts like a jointed rod, but the smoother the joints work, the better will be the stroke.

Another important point for the beginner to keep

in mind is the necessity of preparing for the next stroke the instant the ball has been hit. Do not wait to see where your return is going before you start, but begin instantly to recover your balance and move to the best position for the next stroke. Anticipation of this kind is one of the greatest advantages an experienced player has over the novice.

Footwork. Footwork is the means of perfect weight control and balance, while timing is the transference of the player's weight into his stroke, thus giving "pace" to the ball. Actually, good footwork is the secret of success in boxing, baseball, tennis, football, dancing, and many other sports, for by this medium the punch of the boxer, the carrying power of the batter, the pace of the tennis player, the distance of the punter, or the balance of the dancer is determined. There is a fraction of a second when ball and body are in such a juxtaposition that if the ball is struck then, the speed and pace are increased by the maximum leverage of the body. That is the moment when the weight of the body crosses the centre of balance in a forward movement, and simultaneously the ball in its flight meets the racket. Only by this forward movement of striking the ball is it possible to acquire the maximum power. That is perfect timing.

Good footwork in tennis is as important as sound groundstrokes or a big serve. Without the proper footwork, a player may find his weight moving backward or sideways rather than forward. He may plant his feet too late or too early, block himself glued to the ground when he should be taking a step forward or sideways. Good footwork can mean speed in reaching the ball, balance when meeting it, and power on the hit. The basic requirements for proper tennis footwork are: (1) the weight should be on the balls of the feet rather than the heels; (2) the hop-skip motion should be used when necessary to wind up on the correct foot; and (3) the player should step toward the net with the left foot on the forehand and the right foot on the backhand.

When the player is in the ready position, his weight should be evenly distributed on the toes of both feet. He should feel "bouncy" rather than flatfooted. His feet are well spread and his knees are bent, but he is not leaning over so far that he loses his balance. The "bouncier" he is, the more ready he is to move. When the ball leaves his opponent's racket, he makes his move: he pushes off with his left foot if he is moving toward his right (he lets his weight go onto the heel of his left foot, which is used as the "pusher"). If he does not have far to go, he simply skips sideways, with his body still facing the net. When a ball comes to his backhand, the action is reversed: he pushes off with his right foot to move toward his left. He skips toward balls that he can reach easily by runs toward balls that are wide or very short.

If the opponent hits a short ball that can be reached without difficulty, the player skips forward (the right foot on the forehand is always one step closer to the net than the left). If the ball comes directly to the player rather than to his side, he hop-skips one step toward the backhand so that he can play the ball naturally on his forehand.

The skip is used to prevent a player from getting glued to the ground, to make it easy for his to step toward the net with the proper foot, and to make last-minute adjustments if he misjudged the bounce. The run is always used instead of the skip to reach a difficult ball, but you will often see good players run toward the ball, then skip on the last step (if there is time) so that their footwork will be correct for the hit.

The proper footwork on the hit is neither the open stance with body facing the net not the closed stance with left foot crossing toward the right alley (or right foot crossing toward the left alley).

The wide-open stance does not make it easy to put one's weight into the ball, and the extreme closed stance prevents the weight from moving forward (it is, instead, moving sideways). Correct footwork is to step toward the net—with the left foot on the forehand and the right foot on the backhand. The stance is slightly open on the forehand, but the right side is toward the net on the backhand.

There are times when the player must use the wide-open or the extreme closed stance. One does not have time to adjust footwork against a cannon-ball serve (one simply turns the left shoulder toward the net on the forehand and the right shoulder toward the net on the backhand). Again, when one is running for a very wide ball, one may end up in an extreme closed stance. In the latter case, the shot cannot be an attacking one since the weight is moving in the wrong direction.

If you have been having problems with footwork, review the three basic requirements for the proper approach: (1) on your toes, (2) hop-skip whenever possible, (3) step toward the net with left foot on forehand and right foot on backhand. This may be the answer to bettering your balance and increasing your speed and your power.

Timing. A player with good timing knows when to commence his stroke so that he will meet the ball at the proper moment. A player with poor timing may plan to hit the ball slightly in front of his but may catch it behind him. The two factors which will enable the player to improve his timing are: a consideration of the stroke involved (a forehand is timed differently from a backhand) and very early preparation.

Even if a match is played on a perfect court with no bad bounces, and the opponent hits every ball with exactly the same amount of pace, the player still must adjust his timing to the particular stroke involved. The timing on a groundstroke is different from that on a volley, and the timing on an overhead is different from that on a serve. Forehands are hit a fraction of a second earlier than backhands. Often a player's timing will be "off" on his forehand but perfect on his backhand: occasionally he will have a good backhand day but his forehand will be "off." The stroke did not come apart suddenly: the timing did. The first stage of the cure is to recognize that on backhands, that the timing on volleys is different from that on ground-strokes.

In all strokes one must decide at what point one wishes to meet the ball. The serve should be hit to the side of and slightly in front of the body; volleys should be met 12 to 18 inches in front of the body; groundstrokes should be met several inches in front of the body (for beginners) or several feet in front of the body (for advanced players). Once the desired point of contact is established, the stroke should be practised until this contact is met with more and more regularity. The stroke gets grooved to meet the ball at a particular point.

The easiest way to develop good timing is to play a soft hitter. You are not being rushed and so you can always meet the ball at the point in front of you which you have decided is most desirable. The harder your opponent's pace, the more rapid your preparation must be. One must still try to meet the ball in front of the body, and so the windup must begin as soon as the opponent hits the ball. Never compromise when playing a hare hitter by taking the ball late; keep to the desired point of contact, which is in front of your body.

A change-of-pace artist may throw your timing off. His object is to prevent you from getting a rhythm: he will try to make you hit late by throwing in an occasional hard ball and to make you hit too early by giving you an occasional softer ball. Your own concentration will defeat his strategy of spins, cannonballs, and drop shots since you will be aware immediately of the change in his plan and you can alter your own preparation at once to adjust to the shot.

Awareness of early preparation, the desired point of contact, and your opponent's style will help you develop good timing. This "awareness," which allows you to make adjustments in your own game, will enable you to change from a slow court to a fast one, from soft balls to hard ones, and from ideal conditions to windy ones.

2

TENNIS STROKES

Tennis strokes can be divided into three categories: groundstrokes, volleys, and service strokes. Groundstrokes are those you play after the ball has bounced on your side of the net and include the drive (forehand and backhand), the lob, the drop shot, the half volley, and the overhead smash.

The volley strokes are shots played when the ball is in flight, before it has bounced on your side of the net, and include horizontal volley (forehand and backhand), the overhead volley, the smash, the lob volley and the stop volley.

The service stroke is the one employed to put the ball in play during an actual game. Now let us take a closer look at each of these three categories of strokes.

GROUNDSTROKES

Essentials of the stroke

A sound grip and a firm-wristed swing from the shoulder are essential for a controlled stroke. We strongly recommend the Eastern forehand grip for the beginner as it will itself encourage a firm wrist. Moving your feet so that you get into a sideways-on position parallel to the flight of the ball is also fundamental. From this position you can hit the ball with the most control and power, swinging the racket across the front of the body from hip to hip. Transferring your weight on to your front foot will put your body weight into the stroke.

How to perfect the stroke

The sequence below shows the basic forehand drive played from the back of the court. When copying it, concentrate on your footwork, stepping in with your front foot and keeping far enough from the ball to extend your playing arm when swinging.

As with all tennis strokes there are features of the forehand drive which are especially vital. These key elements, such as the loop, he hitting zone and the follow through, are picked out overleaf so that you can give them particular attention when practising and perfecting your stroke. In a match you will have to play your forehand drive in all sorts of difficult situations, each depending on the speed and direction of your opponent's shot.

Playing the stroke

Prepare for the hit as early as possible taking the racket back level with or slightly below the hitting height and turning your shoulders until your non-hitting shoulder is pointing at the ball. To start the forward swing at the ball you must form a loop with the racket head, letting the elbow of the hitting arm relax so that the forward swing starts from below the hitting height. Step in with your front (left) foot to transfer your weight forward and into the hit. Watch the ball right on to the strings.

Footwork

To position yourself sideways—on to the flight of the

ball turn on your right foot and step in with your left foot.

Improving your stroke

To improve the effectiveness of your basic forehand drive it will help you to study the key elements of the stroke. Particularly note the overall shape of the stroke with the forward swing rising slightly through the hitting zone. Try to develop the feel of lift in the forward swing as this will impart the minimum of topspin to the ball required to keep it from flying beyond your opponent's baseline when hitting the ball hard in attack.

Using the Eastern forehand grip means keeping the wrist particularly firm through the forward swing of the racket. When you first start learning the stroke your natural swing can easily become a slow steering movement which guides the ball where you want but is completely lacking in the necessary racket head speed essential for an attacking forehand. This stiff stroke is common and is often the result of a limited take-back. Play shadow strokes to check the features below.

Joining the take-back and the forward swing with a smooth looping action will increase racket head speed at the hit. This loop forms naturally if you momentarily relax the elbow of your playing arm at the end of the take-back. Under pressure many players fail to do this and keep the arm rigid.

Building the forehand drive into your game

Your opponents will obviously vary the pace and direction of their shots and in the normal course of a match you will have to deal with low, high, wide and short balls. For maximum control you should get to the hitting area as early as possible. Playing wide balls and short balls is shown below. When returning low balls make sure that you bend your knees well, keeping your back straight. Develop a feeling of "sitting" into the ball.

Whenever you are rallying from the back of the court and have to cope with a slow, high bouncing ball, move back during your preparation for the stroke and let the ball fall between shoulder and waist height before stroking upwards through the ball aiming deep towards your opponent's baseline. Lengthen your follow through for control.

Wide ball

1. Begin your run towards the hitting area.
2. Prepare with a shorter take-back than for the basic drive. Brake and pivot on your right foot planting it parallel to the flight of the ball.
3. Transfer your weight on to your front foot, stepping across further than for the shot not played on the run, and swing your racket.
4. After the follow through push off strongly with your right foot and return behind the centremark.

Short ball

1. Run forwards to the approaching ball with quick small steps. Start to take the racket back as you run.
2. Pivot on your right foot opposite where the ball would bounce a second time, getting sideways-on to the flight.

3. Step in parallel to the flight of the ball and swing. You should feel as if you are running through the ball.
4. The rear foot continues through as you move forwards to volley the next return.

Practising on your own

On court you will need as many balls as possible in any suitable container. Take one ball at a time in your non-playing hand and from the ready position behind the centremark on the baseline turn sideways taking the racket back. Drop the ball so that it bounces out to the side and a little in front of you and swing the racket head up to meet the falling ball opposite your leading hip. Repeat this and with each series of balls that you hit concentrate on a separate key element of the stroke. If you are unsure of any feature, try shadow stroking, stopping your racket in the problem area so you can turn your racket in the problem area so you can turn your head and see your error. Incorporate your improvements one at a time by driving dozens of balls.

The best off-court practice is to play drive after drive against some sort of practice wall. You can buy portable practice walls, or you might have access to one, but any sound wall with space in front of it will do. It is best to mark a line 90 cm (3 feet) high along the wall to show the height of the net, and another line 60 cm (2 feet) above this. Stand 4.5 to 6 metres from the wall and aim between the lines. Keep on your toes, returning to the ready position after each stroke before stepping in again for the next hit.

Practising with a partner

If you have a practice partner you can feed balls to each other on court, first dropping balls for the strokemaker, then throwing balls underarm to simulate an opponent's shot. As you gain confidence go to your respective baselines and try to complete 10-, then 20-stroke rallies hitting forehand drives deep into each other's forehand corners as shown right. Good deep shots landing just inside the opposite baseline will keep your opponent away from the net. Keep on your toes and once you are hitting confidently make sure that you move back to your position behind the centremark of the baseline as you would in a game before moving to play the next stroke.

Using your forehand drive

The basic forehand drive is a point and match winner. It is likely that you will play it from the right-hand side of your baseline. You have three choices: to play a drive deep across the court to your opponent's forehand corner; to play a drive deep and parallel to the sideline to your opponent's backhand corner, or to play the ball a little earlier, further in front of your leading hip, in order to hit various angled drives again crosscourt, between the service and baselines.

Forehand drive

the topspin forehand drive is a variant of the basic drive, the difference being the amount of topspin applied to the ball. For the basic drive a minimal amount of topspin is applied, enough to control a hard hit ball on a shallow trajectory. For a topspin drive the more extreme effects of topspin are used to enhance aggressive forehand play.

Deep, effective topspin drives come from preparing for the forward swing early, sound positioning and weight transfer while hitting the ball. Racket face control and combined wrist and forearm action through the hitting zone are also vital for successful topspin driving. The stroke does not depend on a flicking action with the wrist but on a much steeper swing from low to high with the whole arm. As with the basic drive build on a strong swing from the shoulder using the racket as an extension of your wrist and forearm. The same Eastern forehand grip used for the basic forehand drive is suitable for the topspin stroke. If, however, you plan to use the topspin stroke for most of your drives the slightly modified Eastern forehand grip will give more wrist freedom.

Compare the sequence below with that of the basic drive on pages 46 and 47 and you will see the change in the shape of the stroke required for the topspin drive, the racket rising steeply to strike the ball and send it away on a steep, arcing trajectory as shown opposite. It is important tot remember that when playing a topspin shot you can really attack the ball with great racket head speed in the safe knowledge that you are actually hitting control on to the ball. The extra spin applied allows for a greater margin for error than that afforded by the basic stroke as the ball can be sent 1.5 metres or more above the net and it will still and in court.

Comparing topspin forehand drive with the basic version, below, shows how the topspin applied to the ball creates and arcing trajectory, the ball crossing the net at 1.5 metres or more. If you were to hit a basic drive to this height the ball would fly beyond your opponent's baseline, because the ball would lack the speed of rotation through the air. The more spin, the more exaggerated the arc can be. The steep angle of descent will make the ball bounce high and heavy spin makes it shoot forwards after the bounce at your opponent.

The topspinning ball does not float on an even arc. The ball will approach your opponent fast, and will dip to the court sooner than originally seemed the case. The heavily topspin ball will then bound forwards after the bounce at a lesser angle than that at which it approached the court surface, but still steep enough to force the ball higher than it would reach with a basic drive. The exact height and pace of the ball's second flight will depend on the court resistance and surface finish.

The steep forward swing of the racket from low to high for a topspin forehand drive starts with a much deeper loop shape at the end of the take-back than for the basic drive. To accomplish this loop make sure you turn your shoulders fully during the take-back. The racket face is not turned over at the hit as it sometimes appears to be, but remains in a vertical plane until a fraction of a second after the ball has left the racket. To perfect this swing you must maintain the sideways-on to the ball position right into the follow through. To make sure of this it will help to slightly change the angle at which you step in with your front (left) foot. If a line between your front and back foot during a basic drive marked twelve o'clock on an imaginary clock face, then step in towards one o'clock for the topspin drive. This will discourage you from turning in to the net too early in the stroke. At the completion of the stroke your racket arm should finish nearly straight, high and across your body.

Brushing straight up the back of the ball with your racket strings may seem an easier option but will result in poor depth and pace.

Practising on your own

Go on court with as many balls as possible. From your ready position behind the baseline drop balls with the non-playing hand as you did for the basic drive, but this time let the ball drop from higher up so that you can hit the ball at waist level or above after the bounce. Get the feel of applying consistent spin to the ball, watching its trajectory over the net closely so that you can asses your results. To help your confidence, increase the net height to its maximum and then hit several dozen topspin forehand drives across the court and down the sideline. The topspin applied will still give plenty of margin above the net.

When using a practice wall to perfect your topspin drive, mark a line 1.5 metres above net height and aim for just above this line from about 4.5 to 6 metres. The action of topspin will tend to make the ball rise a little as it hits the wall providing a high bouncing rebound.

With a practice partner on court you can play forehand drivers crosscourt to each other as you did when practising the basic forehand drive but this time combine your basic and topspin shots, one player keeping to basic drives and the other to topspin drives. After five minutes switch roles. Your partner can also help you to build a sequence of forehand drives for future use in match play. Get your partner to stand about 3 metres on the other side of the net and throw balls under-arm to your forehand side. Play and repeat the following sequence; I topspin crosscourt drive, 2 basic drive down the sideline, 3 topspin crosscourt angled drive, 4 topspin drive down the sideline.

In match play you will find the topspin forehand drive a considerable bonus. Use it to add variety to your baseline rallying. The greater margin for error and the higher bounce off your opponent's court will combine to apply consistent pressure. It is difficult and tiring to hit flat and powerful drives at shoulder height. Conversely, you will find high bouncing balls easier to attack with a topspin drive. The topspin forehand drive is also a good option for two types of passing shot, one dipping low, passing your approaching opponent at ankle level, and the other passing him high and wide at an angle, always a difficult ball to reach and so difficult to play with any degree of success.

Sliced forehand drive

For the sliced forehand drive the ball is hit in such a way as to achieve a mixture of under-spin and sidespin giving the shot almost opposite characteristics to the topspin drive. The sliced drive was once used extensively in both the men's and women's game, particularly to attack an opponent's weak backhand. It remains a useful variation to add to your repertoire but the stroke is now generally used more sparingly because of rising standards in the top class game. Kurt Nielson, who reached Wimbledon finals in 1953 and 1955 was probably the last top class player in the men's game to use the sliced forehand drive almost exclusively.

Study the differences between the sliced forehand drive and the basic and topspin drives. For the slice the shape of the forward swing of the stroke from high to low around the outside of the ball combines with the racket face angle at the hit to produce the desired underspin. Underspin will tend to make, the ball float and stay airborne longer and so it must be sent low over the net. The ball also tends to slow considerably in flight allowing opponents more time to get set for their replies. This low trajectory and lack of pace can combine to make the ball stay low after the bounce despite its underspin.

Using these characteristics to your advantage requires perfect timing and the ability to choose the right ball to slice. Broadly, you should slice a rising ball because hitting the ball from above net height enables you to put pace into the shot, slicing the ball down into your opponent's court. Hit below net height the sliced drive will rise to clear the net and probably your opponent's baseline too.

Improving your stroke

Pay particular attention to your hitting wrist during the take-back. The height of the racket head at the end of the take-back is achieved by cocking the wrist. There is virtually no loop before the forward swing is started, the racket head being brought forwards and down to meet the ball with the bottom edge of the racket head leading into the hitting zone.

Practising

You can practice the forehand sliced drive on your own by dropping balls from high up for yourself, but it is better to get a practice partner to send you high bouncing balls, either hand fed from about 3 metres on the other side of the net, or by playing topspin forehand drives to you. The high, kicking bounce of the topspin shot makes it an ideal stroke to practice in conjunction with the sliced drive.

Concentrate on hitting down, round and through the ball, and on preventing the racket head from dropping in the low finish.

The shape of the shot

The sliced forehand drive must be hit from above net height wherever possible so that the ball can be hit firmly on a flat trajectory low over the net to bounce deep in your opponent's court. This is in contrast to the arcing trajectories of the basic and topspin drives.

When hit from a similar height to the basic drive, as shown below, the sliced forehand drive is a much weaker shot. The underspin applied to the ball will tend to keep it hanging in the air so the ball must be played close to net height and with little pace so that gravity has time to pull the ball down into court. At the bounce, the low trajectory and lack of pace will combine to keep the ball lower than in a basic drive despite the direction of the ball's spin. A heavily underspin ball hit on a flat trajectory with more pace can be made to bounce up more steeply, at a greater angle than that at which it approached the court surface, but still relatively low.

Using your sliced drive

Slicing the ball requires less energy than the other forehand drives and can be used to preserve stamina in a long match. Suddenly producing a sliced drive during a baseline rally will introduce contrasted flight, pace and bounce for your opponent. The sliced drive with a shortened take-back is particularly useful for returning high, bouncing services at the incoming server's feet. With slight modification the sliced drive can also be used from behind the centre of your baseline to swerve drives wide to your opponent's backhand corner. To accomplish this the sidespin of the stroke is reversed by swinging the racket head from out to in across the back of the ball.

Forehand chop

Like the forehand slice drive, the chop is an underspin stroke but the spin is more heavily applied by the strings biting much more steeply down the back of the ball. Although the ball can be chopped with good control, considerable speed is lost, with the ball tending to hang in the air making it easy prey for a volleying opponent. The underspin will also pose few problems for an aggressive baseline driver.

Technically the forehand chop can best be perfected by using a Continental grip although it can be effectively developed by the Eastern grip player.

Double-handed forehand drive

There have been very few players in the history of tennis who have reached world class using a double-handed forehand drive. Gene Mayer, well up in the world ranking at the moment, is double-handed on both wings. His footwork and positioning, allied to good serving and excellent one-handed volleying, make up for the severe restrictions in reach imposed by double-handed driving. The double-handed forehand stroke can be played with the same variety of spin shown for one-handed driving.

Improving your stroke

Whereas the two-handed backhand drive is played with an unwinding action with both arms fully extended at the hit, the double-handed forehand drive is a cramped stroke played with a winding up action, with the arms slightly bent. As with the one-handed stroke, full power depends on good weight transfer, stepping in with the front as you start the forward swing and getting your weight completely over your front knee at impact and in the follow through. The shape of the swing, as shown below, is similar to the one-handed version.

Backhand drive

The backhand drive is essential to your gem, firstly as the natural complement to your forehand and secondly because match players automatically attack you on your backhand side. Any player is only as strong as his weakest stroke and a poor backhand drive is particularly easy to spot by an alert and proficient opponent.

The backhand drive is played on the opposite side of the body to the forehand, and the ball is consequently hit with the reverse face of the racket. The key components of a good backhand drive are a firm wrist and correct footwork. Once these two major elements have been built into your stroke, you will find it surprisingly easy to master.

The stroke as we know it today is played sideways-on to the ball, instead of from a more square to the net stance which was used in the past and produced defensive, cut strokes. A sideways-on preparation, with your feet parallel to the flight of the ball and your shoulders turned around until your back is almost facing the net, allows you to hit the ball with a winging, lifting movement as you unwind from the take-back. This uncoiling movement is the basis of the modern backhand drive. It is an action which generates considerable power, often greater than that in the forehand drive. This may seem surprising until you consider which part of the body a right-hander would use to break down a door; almost certainly the back of the right shoulder.

The backhand drive demands a change from the Eastern forehand grip, recommended for the forehand, to the Eastern backhand grip. Once you have mastered the backhand grip it is vital to become familiar with changing from forehand to backhand grips, and vice-versa. The approach to perfecting the stroke is similar to that used for the forehand drive and depends on the ability to analyse your own stroke.

Whether you are a beginner simply trying to improve your backhand drive, or whether you are an experienced player who wants to correct a weak backhand, breaking the stroke down into its key components will help.

It is no good concentrating on improving your backhand drive unless you have previously perfected the Eastern backhand grip and the forehand to backhand changeover. The correct grip encourages the economical take-back which is characteristic of the stroke and the wrist firmness required for control. Similarly important is to turn your shoulders (during the preparation of the shot) beyond an imaginary line drawn at right angles to the line of flight.

Like the basic forehand drive the racket path for a

basic backhand drive travels from low to high through the hitting zone, imparting a little topspin to the ball which controls the depth of your shot. This shape is achieved by taking the racket back at about hitting height and making a shallow loop shape with the racket at the end of the take-back. The ball is usually hit a little further in front of your leading hip than for the forehand drive.

Using a full shoulder turn and then stepping in to transfer your weight into the hit should make you feel as though you are cocking and releasing a powerful spring.

When developing the forehand drive you will have learned how to deal particularly with wide and short balls in a baseline rally. The same advice applies for the backhand. Get to the hitting area quickly so that you can play a stroke as close to standard as possible.

Practising on your own

Now that your have mastered the basics of the backhand drive, you should concentrate in your practice sessions on refining each aspect of the stroke until it becomes second nature to perform it correctly. Use the shadow stroke technique which you learned for the forehand drive whenever you feel that you need to correct an error. A practice wall will encourage consistency.

During your practice sessions on court concentrate on improving your ability to alternate between down the sideline and crosscourt shots, as shown right, by simply meeting the ball earlier or later.

Practising with a partner

You will need more time for practising as you now have to include both forehand and backhand drives in the session. Warm up by playing 10-and 20-stroke groundstroke rallies with your partner using both forehand and backhand drives, and down the sideline forehand and backhand drives, each player returning behind the centremark between shots. Finally play competitive rallies with one player playing crosscourt drives while the other puts all his shots down the line, both players hitting forehands and backhands alternately, as shown right. Reverse roles and repeat.

Once you start playing competitively most of your shots will have to be hit on the run. In your practice sessions make sure that you train realistically for match play situations by returning behind the centremark on the baseline between strokes.

When practising drives with a partner, get to the hitting area as quickly as possible preparing your racket as you run. Then place your weight on to your rear foot so that all that remains for the stroke is the step in and swing. This will help to prevent rushing the stroke.

Using your backhand drive

The backhand side of the court is naturally the defensive one but with the development of the modern backhand drive any player has to opportunity to make it an attacking area as well. As with the forehand drive, your usual tactics must be to drive deep to the corners of your opponent's court, as close to the baseline as possible, or to play crosscourt angled shots off your opponent's poorer shots to win the point outright or to force point-winning situations.

TOPSPIN BACKHAND DRIVE

The same difference exists between the nature of the basic backhand drive and the topspin backhand drive as there is between the basic and topspin forehand drives. The gentle topspin that is required to control the length of hard-hit basic drives is dramatically increased for the topspin version so that the characteristic flight and bounce of a ball hit with topspin are exaggerated. These characteristics make the topspin backhand drive an attacking shot.

The development of the topspin backhand drive occurred relatively late in the history of the game when the topspin forehand drive had been in use for some time. But since the Second World War the topspin backhand has been part of most world champions' repertoires from Budge Patty to the incomparable Bjorn Borg. There are many exciting topspin backhand drives on display in today's top class game. Some players practically always use topspin as part of their strategy whereas others reserve it as an attacking alternative. Many develop a wristy, whiplike action to produce topspin but I recommend a stroke which requires the minimum of wrist action and complements the Eastern backhand grip.

Topspin is best added to the basic drive by simply steepening the angle of your forward swing at the ball. The angle of your racket face at the moment of impact should be the same as for the basic drive, although wrist and forearm action will be in the process of turning the racket face forwards.

Because the higher trajectory of the ball in a topspin drive allows it to pass over the net with more room to spare than with a basic drive, it gives you a greater margin for error. Failure to play the stroke correctly—to hit up and through the ball before closing the racket face over—will lead to drives which fall short, or worse still, land in the net.

Practising on your own

With the topspin backhand drive, start, as with the other drives, by going on court with as many balls as possible and dropping them one by one with your non-playing hand, waiting for them to bounce, then stepping in to play the stroke. Make each ball bounce so that you can attack it realistically above waist height. As you have previously mastered basic backhand driving you should simply be concerned with the differences in technique required for topspinning. Shadow stroke without hitting balls, stopping to check any of the key features of the stroke which you may suspect, but always work improvements into the complete stroke as soon as possible by driving balls down the sideline and crosscourt. You can, of course, use a practice wall to great benefit as for the other drives.

Practising with a partner

Starting from the baseline rally position, with your partner supplying good height balls to you by hand, run out and play your topspin backhand drive crosscourt, returning behind the centremark between each shot. Swop roles with your partner and when you are both playing the stroke well, progress to rallying corner to corner. Then alternate strokes with your partner, first you hitting topspin drives and your partner basic drives, then vice-versa, for ten minutes each way.

You can then move on to the sequence shown right, with one of you hitting basic forehands and backhands crosscourt while the other plays topspin forehands and backhands down the sideline. Once you are both coping well, introduce points scoring. The player who wins a rally by forcing an error from the other wins a point, and then starts the next rally. When one of you reaches 11 points, swop roles playing topspin drives for one set of points and basic drives for the next.

Using your topspin backhand drive

The inclusion of the topspin backhand drive in your choice of strokes will especially help you to counter-attack when your opponent comes in to the net as you can produce dipping returns to the feet. It will also help you to return and approach shot which draws you wide to the backhand as you can now produce a topspin passing shot.

The topspin alternative will help you to keep your opponent guessing; however, beware of producing short length balls. Make sure that your shots penetrate after the bounce by applying enough pace.

To become a complete tennis player you need to include the backhand slice drive in your choice of strokes. Unless, however, you can develop it in the way Ken Rosewall did you should look on the slice as a useful variation to your basic and topspin drives and certainly not as a replacement for either.

A ball hit with underspin tends to hang in the air, and if it is not hit on a flat trajectory, to bounce up without forward momentum. Such characteristics are clearly defensive and in keeping with the more naturally defensive backhand side. The backhand slice drive retains a respectability in top class tennis (especially in the women's game) that the forehand slice has lost. At their best, Britain's Wimbledon champions, Ann Jones and Virginia Wade, were both very adept at the backhand slice. American player Kathy Jordan has an effective defensive backhand slice drive as do many other women on the present world circuit.

As shown on the forehand slice underspin is hit on to the ball by combining a high to low swing with a controlled open racket face at the point of impact. So as to counteract the disadvantages of a long, floating flight and an easy bounce, it is best to slice high bouncing balls, especially ones which are still rising. This will allow you to hit the ball hard, on a flat trajectory, low over the net. Lower balls hit with the same strength may fly out of court unless hit with sidespin.

Improving your stroke

The shape of the forehand slice drive will show you the high to low line of the forward swing for your backhand slice drive. The standard spin for a slice backhand drive is shown on the ball below. To achieve this mixture of sidespin and underspin your racket face must hit down, through and around the ball in the direction of the arrow. It will help to take the racket back with the face more open (bottom edge leading) than in the basic drive preparation. Make sure that after the hit you do not let the racket head fall away but rather rise again after the descent through the ball.

Using an alternative slice

The slight sidespin which the standard backhand slice drive carries as a result of hitting around the outside, as well as through and underneath, the ball ensures at least a straight flight if not one that curves in towards the middle of the court. This is the shot which you should use as a regular variant to your basic and topspin drives. There is, however, a way of sidespinning the ball in the direction shown, below, by preparing your racket further away from your body and then hitting inside the line of flight. Keeping the racket face open as for the standard shot, the out to in swing will draw the strings across the back of the ball.

Practising on your own

Practice the stroke on court by dropping balls with your non-playing hand. Smooth out any imperfections in your technique by shadow stroking as you have done for the other drives. Always go back to driving batches of balls to test your results. Watch the flight of your practice shots carefully, making sure that the balls travel lower over the net band than for a basic drive and deep towards the opposing baseline on a flat trajectory. Experiment with a batch of balls hit with the alternative outward swerving shot shown above right, and finish your session by playing your new stroke in sequences with the other backhand drives that you have learned.

Practising with a partner

"Alley driving" or "tramline hitting", is a very useful practice for developing controlled power once you have mastered the basics of a groundstroke. Use the narrow band of court between the singles and doubles sidelines as your full court, and with your partner opposed to you at the other end, shown right, practice your backhand slice drive while he or she improves their forehand drives. Balls must land in the alley area to count. Basic, topspin or slice drives, or all three at once, can be practised in this way. After 15 minutes, change ends or use the other alley, and switch roles. Try to keep 20-shot rallies going, or play for points.

Backhand drive

The strategic value of the slice when rallying against the baseliner is that its introduction into a rally adds variety to your play posing different problems for your opponent so that it is difficult for him to achieve a settled hitting rhythm. The effectively sliced ball skids through low after the bounce. Aim for this result and use the stroke against rising topspin balls at waist height. Mix in the alternative out-to-in slice.

As with the forehand stroke, the backhand slice with a shortened preparation can be used as a controlled approach shot. Its prolonged flight will give you more time to gain a good volleying position. Make sure that you choose shorter, poor length balls.

Avoid using the slice drive as a passing shot because underspin will keep the ball in the air, making it easy for your opponent to volley.

Backhand chop

the backhand chop is a similar stroke to the backhand slice drive but is more compact and applies fiercer underspin to the ball. The path of the racket is steep from high to low in a chopping action, so that the angle between the racket face and ball through the hitting zone manufactures the heavy spin. The characteristics of a ball hit with underspin are even more accentuated in the chop making the ball sit up rather than shoot through low so its use is more limited than the slice drive in baseline rallies unless your opponent is particularly susceptible to a floating, slow bouncing ball.

Pick balls which bounce above net height so that you can chop them aggressively, deep into your opponent's court. If you chop balls which have fallen below net height you will have to hit them without pace to make them fall short of your opponent's baseline.

Improving your stroke

The preparation for the chop should be high, with the bottom edge of the racket face slightly leading, but make it shorter than for the backhand slice. Simply uncock your wrist as you bring the racket head down. Meet the ball ahead of your leading hip, hitting down and slightly across the back of the ball to apply some sidespin for extra control.

Using your backhand chop

As with the forehand stroke, the backhand chop is a stroke to be used sparingly during baseline rallies with a view to breaking an opponent's rhythm. You should only use it more frequently when your opponent shows himself inept at dealing with the chopped ball. The chopped return is sometimes an effective foil to high bouncing, topspin shots, and if used as such, should be chopped deep to your opponent's baseline. If you are tired during a match remember that the chop requires a minimum amount of energy and precise footwork is less vital than for other strokes. So for defensive purposes alone the backhand chop is a worth while stroke to include in your game.

The compactness of the backhand chop and its tolerance of imprecise footwork makes it useful for returning service especially against topspin services when the receiver can chip the ball to the feet of the incoming volleyer.

Double-handed backhand drive

Playing the backhand drive with two hands on the racket grip strengthens the hitting and control of very young players and often seems quite natural. Other players find the extra hand on the grip allows them to play topspin backhand shots more easily.

Your two-handed grip will determine the development of your stroke. Your dominant hand should hold the racket grip at the butt end and the supporting hand should nestle above it, using the grip, below. Release your support hand for wide balls.

Improving your stroke

The shape of the basic double-handed backhand drive should be similar to the one-handed version. The double-handed stroke requires shoulder turn and body rotation, especially through the hitting zone. Changing your grip, shown right, takes place during the first step of preparation as you turn from your ready position. Most double-handers stand in the ready position with the supporting hand, not at the throat of the racket as usual, but lower on the shaft and with the backhand grip lightly formed.

As you take the racket head down slightly making a shallow loop before you swing upwards through the ball. Such a racket path will apply enough controlling topspin to limit the length of your drives. Transfer your weight on to your front foot as you make the shot and make sure that you unwind through the forward swing. Extend your arms at the hit and finish about head height.

DROPSHOTS

The dropshot family of strokes encompasses the short-range shots played after the ball has bounced and designed to fall short of your opponent. The basic forehand and backhand dropshots, shown below, are played with underspin. Variations, shown overleaf, are the dink shot, which is usually played with topspin, and the dump shot, which is a simple push through the ball from the forecourt normally played against balls above net height. All dropshots can be played with your driving grips.

Dropshot play is exciting and full of suspense, especially on grass courts where the ball dies quickly. Its success depends on surprising your opponent so that it is very difficult for him to recover and play the ball which you have placed only a metre or two over the net. You can often use the similarity between the dropshot and sliced drive preparations to disguise your intentions when playing the basic dropshots. You can also use the two varieties of the dropshot, shown below, the dink shot and the dump shot. Having previously learned the topspin drives, the soft topspin forehand and backhand dink shots should come easily enough to you. You will find the dink shot is especially effective when played from near the service line but it can also be played with underspin or sidespin from no man's land. The dump is played from quite near the net, with your body weight almost static, against higher balls which can be placed over the net.

Practising on your own

On one side of the net place targets opposite each other on the sidelines, one pair 1.5 metres from the net, and another pair 3 metres from the net. Firstly, take up a position just inside the service line on the other side of the net with your basket of balls. Drop balls for yourself practising both forehand and backhand dropshots using the targets to assess your accuracy. Persevere until you get 75 per cent of your balls to bounce gently between the 1.5 metre targets and the net, and the remainder short of the 3 metre targets. You can then move back a metre for your next basket of balls, and finally to just inside your baseline. If you have the use of a practice wall, mark a line on the ground 1.5 metres from it. Retire to your usual driving position 4.5 to 6 metres from the wall and play and repeat drive followed by dropshot, as shown right, aiming to make the ball fall between the 1.5 metre line and the wall with every dropshot.

Using your dropshots

In match play, adopt the mental rule that your dropshots will never fall on your own side of the net. Giving yourself this margin for error will mean that, at the outset, your dropshots will be forcing weak returns from your opponent rather than winning points outright. This is far better than being dispirited by the sight of an overambitious dropshot falling into the net. Generally, play dropshots against medium paced balls, aiming to the side of the court as far away as possible from your stranded opponent. If there is no advantage in playing to either side, aim for the middle of the court so that the ball travels over the lowest part of the net. Dink shots, and dump shots played from closer the net, should be similarly used but remember that the dink shots can be usefully directed towards opponents' feet when they are approaching the net.

The forehand drive "off the ground" is the commonest stroke in the game, so you should learn to make it before you go on to any other. It is the foundation of both attack and defence; and it must be thoroughly mastered if you are to become a good player.

It is the commonest stroke in the game because, first, the number of strokes off the ground is never less than 50 percent even when both players are volleyers by temperament, and rises to considerably over 90 percent when both players are base-liners; and second, because three-quarters of all these groundstrokes are forehand strokes, owing to everybody's natural preference for, if possible, taking the ball forehanded rather than backhanded. The purpose of the forehand is to return a ball on the racket side of the body (the right side of a righthanded player or the left of a lefthanded player) after it has bounced once. It should be used to keep the ball and the opponent deep in the opposite court. That is, a deep drove into your opponent's court gives you more time to reach the net and materially reduces the possibility of being successfully passed or lobbed. To accomplish this, a ball hit by the forehand drive must be placed near the top of the net (low), near the opponent's base line (deep), and should carry speed (flat or topspin). Fortunately, this most important stroke is the easiest and the most natural to learn.

To make a forehand stroke properly, it is most important to get into the proper position to hit the ball right. This means to run to a position in the court about 2 or 3 feet to the left of where the ball will come up from its bound. You should be well back of the spot where it hits the ground so as to allow room for the bound, and also to permit you to meet it as your weight is thrown forward or toward the ball itself. When this position is reached your left foot should be forward or toward the net and the right back of it nearly in direct line with the flight of the ball.

As you ball strikes the ground, your racket should start to move in the backswing, and should pass around behind your body and slightly upward, extended at the full reach of the arm. As previously stated, most beginners find it very difficult to start the backswing early enough, and a late start shortens the backswing and makes the stroke jerky and poorly executed, lacking power. In the forehand drive, the swing should be as continuous as possible, with no stopping of the racket at the end of the backswing, but a slight turn and an immediate forward swing without checking the headway of the racket. To pull back the racket only a foot or so, stop it to gauge the flight of the ball, and then start it forward to hit will never accomplish anything in tennis. The momentum of the racket must be kept up from the start back until long after the ball has been hit, for that, not the strength in the arm, is what gives power to the stroke.

The racket should act as simply an extension of the forearm, and be kept as far away from the body as possible. The upper arm, forearm, and racket all three act as a jointed rod that strikes like a flail, and if the wrist is added to the movement it becomes like a whiplash in its action, imparting a powerful blow. At all times avoid getting your elbow cramped up close to the body. As the backswing is made the body should be turned or pivoted around on the hips and both the shoulders and the hips turned to follow the racket back and make its swing easier. The weight should be evenly balanced between the two legs when the backswing is started and then transferred back onto the right foot to carry the weight back evenly without losing balance.

As the ball starts to rise from the ground, the forward, or hitting, swing starts, and the unwinding of the backward coil reverses its first action. The hips turn first, then the shoulders, followed by the upper arm, forearm, and wrist as the racket sweeps forward to meet the ball. In this forward swing, the weight is again shifted back from the right foot to the even centre when the ball is met and then continued on until it ends entirely on the left foot.

The ball should be met at a height between the knee and waist and as nearly as possible opposite the centre of the body. The racket must be guided so that the ball strikes the centre of the stings of the racket, the nearer the centre the better. Meeting the ball off centre is likely to turn the racket in the hand and always reduces the strength as well as the accuracy of the shot.

The head of the racket should be perpendicular to the ground at the moment when the ball is hit—that is, the top part of the frame should be no farther forward or back than the lower part. This gives what is known as an "open" racket and the greatest accuracy and strength in the stroke. The handle of the racket should be very nearly parallel to the ground.

From the point of impact, there are three variations of the end of the stroke, all having their own uses and advantages, and the player can select any style he pleases, and vary the style of shot, if he can control several styles, for different results.

The flat forehand drive. The ideal forehand drive is a flat drive skims the net and yet is able to keep your opponent deep in his court. But flat drives are too difficult to control, especially on low bounces; for if the ball crosses the net higher than 6 inches or so above the net cord, it will land out of court. This margin of safety is too small. Topspin, on the other hand, enables you to drive the ball 2 or more feet above the net and also deep to your opponent's base line. Your margin of safety above the net is much greater than with the flat drive; and the forward downspin, aided by gravitation, pulls the ball downward within the court after it has crossed the net. You should therefore make fewer errors.

The term *flat* as it is used in tennis means a ball hit without spin. A ball hit *totally* without twist or spin would naturally travel in the same direction in which it stars until its momentum is spent and gravity alters its course. But it is almost impossible to hit a tennis ball without giving it some spinning motion. The strings of the racket cling very close to its rough surface, and the slightest motion of the racket that is off the straight line tends to wipe or brush them across the surface of the ball, and makes it revolve before it loses contact.

Topspin on the forehand. Topspin enable a player to hit with more pace, depth, and control. A stroke without spin depends on gravity alone to bring he ball into court. Topspin makes a hard-hit ball dip after it clears the net comfortably; under the same circumstances, a flat ball would sail out. A stroke with topspin is the ideal passing shot since the spin pushes the ball down, thus forcing the volleyer to hit a low ball; a stroke with underspin is the most dangerous passing shot since the underspin causes the ball to rise, thus allowing the volleyer to down on a high ball.

In topspin (or overspin or loop), the top edge of the tennis ball is turning in the direction of the opponent while the bottom edge is moving away from him. In underspin (or backspin), the bottom edge of the ball is spinning toward the opponent. The topspin ball tends to drop to the ground faster than a ball without spin, while the underspin ball tends to hang in the air.

Topspin is achieved by the upward motion of the racket with respect to the ball. Therefore the racket must approach the ball from below ball level (this does not mean that the racket head should be dropped). A player can still take a high backswing if he so chooses, but he must then develop a circular so that his racket will be below ball level just before the hit. The racket face can be either slightly closed, absolutely perpendicular to the ground, or slightly open. However, if the face is too closed, the ball will go short or into the net; if the face is too open, the player will have to pull up sharply with his racket (use an enormous amount of topspin) to bring the ball into court.

The follow-through on a topspin shot must be higher than the level at which the ball is hit. In other words, the racket starts below ball level and ends above ball level. It is not necessary to roll the face of the racket over after the ball has been hit. This action has not effect on the ball since the moment of impact is already over. Some players do roll the face of the racket over, but it is just a matter of personal idiosyncrasy—just as a big backswing or a small backswing are matters of personal idiosyncrasy.

Players with Eastern, Western, or Continental grips can bit topspin shots. The Continental grip is usually hit with a cocked wrist (the racket head points upward). Continental players who try topspin will pull up sharply with the arm as the ball is h it. The movement is therefore upward rather than forward, and this makes for a rather erratic action. In the Western style, the wrist is laid way back, the elbow is bent, and the racket ends up very high. The topspin is pronounced, but the grip makes it difficult to handle low balls because the wrist must be bent around so much. The Eastern grip is ideal for the topspin shot since it can be used on low, medium, or high balls. The wrist is laid back on the backswing but is firm at the moment if impact. Beginners and intermediates should use as little wrist action as possible since topspin with the Eastern grip can be achieved by racket trajectory alone (the racket starts below ball level and ends above ball level). Wrist action or wrist snap can be developed later by good players who want to add a little variety to their game.

The amount of topspin given to any shot depends to a degree on the hitting position of the ball. For example, a ball that is higher than the waist (which is higher than the net) requires less spin and can be hit almost flat. But when a ball is lower than the waist (below the net), it requires some lifting. Where one has to lift, one is required to put something on the ball to bring it down again. Thus more topspin is required on a low shot than on a high one. To do this, the face of the racket must be kept slightly open (you must reconcile the angle of your racket face with the angle of your hitting), and you must start your stroke lower than where the ball will be hit. In other words, you use topspin in different degrees as the situation demands to control shots. This knowledge comes only by trial and error and plenty of practice.

Slice and chop strokes. There is still a third variation of making the forehand groundstroke with an underspin or backspin. The predominating feature of these is the underspin on the ball that is importer, for a slice stoke (sometimes ca., a *cut shot*) or chop stroke always makes the ball spin *backward* in a direction opposite to that used in the drop stroke. The spinning motion is against the flight of the ball through the air, the top moving backward and the bottom forward, which is again exactly opposite to what happens when the topspin is used.

All of these strokes are made by striking the ball with a glancing blow, the bottom edge of the racket being forward and the strings touching more of the under side of the ball than the top. In order to prevent such a blow underneath from lifting the ball up too high, the swing must be made with a downward angle. The racket starts high and ends low, very different from the drop stroke, and the head is dragged across the ball sharply while the strings are still in contact with its cover.

The chop stroke is used primarily as a defensive

weapon to change the pace of the game, or against a player who does not like to run or to handle a stroke with spin. There are two distinct types of chop shots: the deep chop and the soft chop.

The deep chop, or underspin drive, is used as a change upon the topspin drive and is played from the same position on the court. This chop also is highly effective as a means of returning the wide-bounding American twist service. As a rule, you should restrict its use to only high-bounding balls where you have a straight angle down over the net. On low-bounding balls, those below the level of the net, this shot has the tendency to sail out of the court.

The soft chop shot (known also as the *drink* or *softie*) is used only when you are up close (never more than 5 feet from the net) and your opponent is playing deep. Then it is aimed to drop closely over the net and should be played on a cross-court angle. For if you play it straight down the court, nine out of ten times the shot will go too deep and be recovered. Therefore, you angle the ball away from your opponent.

In making the chop stroke, the player crouches even more than in any of the other strokes, the bend from the hips forward being more pronounced. The racket is swung back slower than in the drop shot and not nearly so far. Few of the slice-stroke players carry their rackets in the preliminary swing back farther than behind the shoulder. As the swing is shorter, it can be made later with greater accuracy than with the drop shot. This is the feature that generally appeals to beginners, the short swing, and many adopt the chop-stoke style at first and change afterward when they learn of its limitations. It is much wiser to begin with the other stroke and learn that properly to avoid the necessary change in style later.

The position of the feet for the chop stroke also is slightly different from the others, as the shorter swing does not depend so much on momentum, and the right foot is extended as a rule farther forward to steady the player as he strikes. This stroke is made off the right foot, while the drop stroke is made off both feet, the weight being pretty equally divided during the stroke. As the racket is brought sharply down to meet the ball, the shoulders straighten up a little to take some of the bend out of the elbow, but at no time in the stroke is the arm as straight as in the other strokes. There is an inclination to bend the elbow somewhat in making all chop strokes, and this bend is not fully straightened out with most players until the very end of the stroke.

When the ball is met, all of the body weight is suddenly exerted in the racket, the shoulders doing more than the hips, and the wrist adds to the "drag" of the racket across the ball to five it the necessary twist. As the stroke is finished, all of the weight is thrown over to the forward foot and the arm and racket end their swing with the downward thrust still further pronounced. The racket finishes out in front of the left knee, extended at the full length of the arm, and the shoulders turned around completely in their effort to check its swing without losing the balance.

The greatest difficulty the player has to overcome in using the chop stroke is its tendency to drive the ball out of court. In order to prevent this, the stroke must be played slower and with less power so it will not go too far, and this necessity robs the stroke of the virtue of speed that other strokes possess. As against this drawback, however, it must be conceded that the short backswing and the more constrained position permit greater accuracy, and as a rule chop-stroke players have a closer control of their slow returns than do drop-stroke players of their faster shots. The player can delay longer before striking, and this allows him to change in the opponent's position makes it necessary.

On the other hand again, it is much easier for the opposing player to volley an undercut ball at the net than a drop shot, for its underspinning motion makes the ball twist downward and go away from his racket faster. The revolution of a top-spinning ball tends to make it leave a volleyer's racket slower and jump upward when volleyed. For this reason, the cut strokes are less effective against an opponent who is at the net ready to volley, and the drop strokes are the best against such an opponent. Conversely, the drop stroke is best against a net player and weakest against an opponent at the back of his court.

It is a distinct advantage to play the ball from as high in the air as possible, but the upward motion of the racket makes it difficult to do this when making a drop shot. The motion of the racket in the chop stroke just reverses this, being in the downward direction, so that these strokes can be played from a much higher bound than the others.

Often the disadvantage of the underspin which keeps the ball up in its flight can be overcome by striking it from a higher point and consequently closer to the net, which will sometimes take the volleyer by surprise and pass him with the slower ball this stroke affords, because it is played with more of a downward angle which allows it to travel nearly as fast as the other and still remain inside the court lines. The slice, or side-twist shot, causes the ball to bounce low and to curve to the side on which the spin is applied. It can be hit either forehand or backhand and is good on low-bounding balls. Actually, the slice and chop are executed in exactly the same manner from the standpoint of grip, position, and stance. However, in the slice, instead of hitting down on the back of the ball, you hit down and to the outside of it, imparting under and sidespin. When making the forward swing fro a forehand slice, the racket, starting outside and above the ball, is brought down through the air at an angle almost 45 degrees to your left, and as it moves in this almost forward-sideward diagonal path, the racket cuts across the bottom of the ball. This severe right-to-left cut causes the ball to curve to your right. For the backhand slice, the cut is from the left to your right, which causes the ball to rotate in the same direction and curve in its flight to your left. As you could expect, these strokes require strong wrist action, an open-face racket, and a follow-through that will extend naturally in the direction of the shot.

Some players succeed in using side twists with either a topspinning or an undercut ball. When hit with a horizontal racket these are only possible by advancing the wrist well ahead of the ball and drawing the racket in toward the body while in contact, which gives the ball an out twist as well as an underspin or a topspin according to whether the racket travels upward or downward when it meets the ball. These side twists are used most in the services, however, which are made with a racket that is more nearly perpendicular, and therefore allows the motion to be sidewise without interfering with the body swing, by the use of the wrist. This will be taken up later in this section under the heading of Services.

The backspinning shots, both of them, carry less speed than the flat-hit or the topspinning shot and are therefore more used for defence than for attack. But with any tennis stroke, do not try for speed in your drives until you have mastered the stroke. Remember, in tennis, science is often more important than strength. Do not try to "knock the cover off the ball," or "blast your opponent off the court." Placing the ball in the right spot at the right time is more important. Actually, learning to drive a tennis ball fast is something like driving an automobile. You will come to grief if you drive at eighty miles per hour before you have learned to control the car at a speed of forty. Apply the same principle when learning to drive a tennis ball. If you are a beginner, do not drive too fast. As your control improves. Gradually increase your speed. When you have so mastered the forehand stroke that you do not need to think about your footwork or your swing, then drive as fast as you like, provided you further that increased speed warrants the increased risk. Therefore, as you develop your forehand, concentrate first on control. Power, speed, and deception will come naturally, if you learn first the fundamentals of control.

Backhand groundstrokes

The backhand groundstrokes are used to return balls which have bounced once on the court to the left of a righthanded player or to the right of a lefthander. Their importance cannot be overemphasized. The opportunity of playing the backhand drive should never be avoided by moving position to play the ball on your stronger and generally more reliable forehand. Such a practice not only reveals a major weakness to your opponent, but also leaves an area of the court unprotected. In other words, one may prefer the forehand stroke and use it on every possible occasion, but no chain is stronger than its weakest link, and if there is a distinct weakness in the backhand play, the defence will be vulnerable whenever attacked by a "heady" player.

There is no question that the forehand stroke is the easier way to play the ball. It is the natural way, and the arm and elbow are less embarrassed when swinging the racket on the right side of the body that when they must be crossed over to reach a ball on the other side. That is, in forehand play, the backswing is clear of the body and the turn as the blow is delivered keeps the arm free, but in backhand play the arm must swing across the body, and the pushing muscles of the upper arm rather than those that pull are used in making the stroke. The grip of the hand too allows all the power to be *behind* the racket for a forehand shot, while on the other side the necessary grip forces the hand *above,* and in the Continental more of a pull than a push. The shoulder is seldom behind the ball and the turning of the body for the follow-through is never so pronounced in backhand play, because the striking arm is already far advanced when the stroke begins and it is difficult to shift so that the ball can be followed as long as in forehand play.

The methods of gripping the racket, which vary distinctly for this stroke from all the others, have been fully covered earlier in this section, and the general elements of good form also bear strongly on this stroke. But in addition to these, there are a good many points which apply only to backhand strokes; the beginner should study these carefully before going deeper into the play.

As in the forehand stroke, there are the same options regarding the best way of hitting the ball and the exact amount of twist of put on it. One can play the ball nearly straight with little or no twist, by using a perfectly straight follow-through; he can put topspin on the ball and give it the same dropping tendency already recommended for the forehand stroke, or he can use a chop stroke that will make the ball spin backward in its flight through the air.

In the backhand stroke the proper stance and backswing should be coordinated even more closely than in the forehand. From the anticipatory or readiness position, with the right hand relaxed on the handle and the left lightly cradling the throat, you begin the backswing of your body and racket immediately when the ball is seen to be coming toward your backhand. Start the stroke by turning your right shoulder toward the net. This turning movement begins as the racket head starts swinging back at hip level. The left hand guides the racket back and the right hand makes a change to the backhand grip. With the racket still coming back, pivot to the left on the ball of your left foot. As the backswing nears its completion, the racket should be well back and behind you, knees flexed, the eyes and head forward, and the body and shoulders rotated away from the net. Actually, your body should be swung around to the left far enough so that your back is almost half turned to it. Watch the flight of the oncoming ball over your right shoulder and keep the racket head above the wrist at all times during the backswing. The weight of your body should be on the back, or left foot. Thus, the pivot in the backhand stroke is much more emphatic than in the forehand drive. Many inexperience players do not turn their bodies nearly enough; in consequence, the racket arm meets with resistance by not being able to swing past the body. If there is any doubt of the importance of the turn of the body, stand sideways facing the net and, without turning the body, see how far the racket can be taken back. Then try it again, but on this occasion turn your hips away from the net, and you will quickly find that your racket arm has a much smoother swing. During the backswing, the racket's path can be either an almost horizontal flat arc kept at hip level on its trip back or it can be circular with its peak at about shoulder height and with the racket head tilted slightly backward. The flat-arc backswing, similar to the horizontal straight-back motion in the forehand stroke, is usually recommended for beginners. Once you have the footwork and timing mastered, you can use the circular backswing. But with either backswing, the left hand should be kept on the racket until you start the forward swing.

In the completed backswing position your weight is back on the rear foot, left knee loose and bent, right knee sagged; and you are looking over your right shoulder, eyes glued on the oncoming ball. Having "wound" yourself up into such a position, you must now reverse the action into and through the ball. Release the left hand from the throat of the racket and swing the right arm and racket toward the net in an almost flat arc in line with the oncoming ball or slightly below it. In the latter case, the racket head will help to give the ball its necessary topspin, but do not exaggerate the upward movement or too much spin will occur. As the racket comes closer to the point of impact, the weight of the body is gradually transferred to the front, right foot. Your wrist should be straight and your elbow kept slightly bent and close to your body until the ball has been hit. The ball should be met at a point from 10 to 15 inches in advance of the right hip and the right hip should be drawn in. The mechanics of the backhand drive make it next to impossible to execute the shot consistently unless impact occurs before the ball reaches a point opposite the body. Actually, there is no feature in connection with the execution of any stroke in tennis as important as this. Also keep away from the ball. All too many players hit the ball with a backhand stroke too close to the body, which cramps the shot and results in less power and speed. Keeping away from the ball makes for free, confident, hard hitting and will materially help to eliminate errors. At the moment of impact, the complete momentum of your swing should have reached its maximum speed with the body turned into the ball by swinging the left shoulder well around. The weight of the body should now all be on the right foot. The knee should be bent while the left knee should be sagged and turned inward, with the rear foot steadying your body for balance. Do not use any type of push-off action with this foot to help the shop. Your grip should be gradually tightening on the racket handle so that at impact the wrist is firm or locked. Your arm should be straightened well out from the body as you swing through the ball.

While it is best to stroke a ball at waist level, your opponents do not always oblige by hitting the ball so that it bounces to this height. Therefore, you must learn to make the backhand swing at all levels. For a low shot, one below waist level, you follow the same procedure as for low forehand strokes. That is, you bend your knees so that you bring your waist level down to the level of the ball. Except for the bending of the knees, the backhand stroke is executed in the same manner as that used on a waist-level ball. For balls that have a very low bounce, those just off your shoe top, the hitting should be a little upward, with the racket face slightly tilted back. This open face will lift the ball to the proper height over the net. Remember that it is usually advantageous to hit the ball on the rise—at least it should be hit before it begins to fall. This means that you opponent will have less time to get into position and your shot may be concealed to a greater extent.

Topspin and underspin. Topspin and backspin can be applied to backhand drives. The topspin backhand starts low and ends high; the underspin backhand starts high and ends low. In the topspin shot, the face of the racket is perpendicular to the ground at the moment of impact; in the underspin or slice shot, the racket face is open at the hit. That is, by rolling the racket backward and allowing the racket to pass under the ball, a backspin is given, and we have an undercut that has a tendency to keep the ball up in the air long and make its bound low. It is a good stroke for straight side-line shots, when the distance to the base line or diagonally to where the ball would go out of court is so long that the stroke can be played fast without danger; but for cross-court shots it is generally difficult to play fast and hold in court. This stroke is easy to volley at the net, too, so that it is seldom as good a passing stroke against a volleyer. With the opponent at the base line, however, when only driving must be considered, it is very useful, because its slow "hop" is a mean, lifeless ball to handle off the ground.

For the chop and slice stroke, the racket should finish low, generally at about the height of the waist, but for the topspinning, rolling lift stroke, the racket's swing should end much higher, generally above the shoulder. The same principles of meeting the ball and imparting the twist apply as in the forehand stroke, and some experts get the same variations here by increasing their follow-through and imparting the twist with a turn of the wrist at the last moment before the ball leaves the racket.

As the player becomes better and the competition stiffer, he will find it more difficult to hit backhand topspin shots down the line. The ball is coming hard and deep, and if the player's preparation if the least bit late, he will err on the down-the-line. He therefore has two choices: to slice or to prepare earlier. The latter is the wiser decision although frequently he will slice for better control. But the backhand stroke without any twist at all, the straight hit ball, is perhaps more valuable for general play than either of the others. As in forehand drives, however, control is the most important consideration in your backhand stroke production. Uncontrolled speed loses more points than it wins; it is where you place the ball that counts.

LOBBING

The lob was, originally, almost entirely a defensive groundstroke. It consists of hitting the ball up high in the air, so that it will pass high over the head of your opponent if he is forward in the court and drop far back by his base line. It was, and still is, of great use in getting yourself out of a disadvantageous position and giving you time to assume an advantageous one, or perhaps only to give you breathing time, if you are being run about a great deal from one end to the other of your base line. Its two main object are to drive your opponent away from the net and to enable you to get there yourself. To attain these objects, two kinds of lob are in use: the fast, comparatively low, one, which is played just over the top of your opponent's reach; and the high toss, which is intended to hit right at the back of his court. There is one essential common to both forms: they must be deep. You must aim to hit right on his base line, or at most a foot inside it. A short lob is, or ought to be, fatal. The most useful lob is one to your opponent's backhand corner; but, of course, you should not lob repeatedly to the same place.

The development of the lob into an effective weapon of attack was introduced by American international players in the late 1920s. Actually, it is a valuable means of dislodging a volleyer from the net. No volleyer can stay at the net against a good lob, and there are very few players who can smash a deep lob, or, at any rate, who can go on doing so. Sooner or later the strain of watching—and hitting—the ball tells; the ball goes into the net, and the patient lobber gets his reward.

Like other groundstrokes, lobe can be made either forehand or backhand. In addition, many of the same rules apply here as in the groundstroke drives. The ball must not be taken in front of the body, nor with the wrong foot or shoulder forward. The body should be turned with the side toward the net to allow a full swing as in a good drive and the same freedom of the arm and shoulder is required.

The lob is a slower stroke and much more deliberate than any other groundstroke. The backswing is shorter and the body motion in the actual stroke less pronounced, while the follow-through is very much reduce. The racket should be dropped with the head distinctly below the wrist, and the stroke has an upward swing that is absent in the other groundstroke. With the head of the racket hanging downward at an angle of 45 degrees, the same free sweep of the arm is made, with the ball well off to the side so that the shoulder can be brought into the stroke.

The sweep of the racket must be long and smooth, not jerky like the stab of a chop stroke. The ball is met with even less impact than in other groundstrokes and is swept away rather than hit with a sharp blow. The slower the stroke can be made, the better are the results likely to be. No other stroke in the game is made with such deliberate movements.

The most dangerous error for the beginner to counteract, however, is the desire to strike the ball from underneath and drive it straight upward in the air. On the contrary, the ball must be hit clearly from behind, with a forward sweep, the upward turn coming just before the racket meets the ball. The bevel of the face of the racket can be depended on almost as much as the upward swing to direct the ball high enough to pass over the opponent's head. Except when it is played for the purpose of gaining time to recover position in court or to get a resting spell when the player is hard pressed, a lob should not be driven any higher in the air than is necessary to keep clear of the opponent's reach. With the other man at the net ready to smash, which is generally his position when the lob is used, it is only necessary for the ball to pass a foot or two above the highest point he can reach by jumping, and the lower it can safely pass him the better. If only a little out of reach, the stroke will have a flatter trajectory and more forward motion on the ball, and will greatly reduce the other man's chances of turning and running back to make the return.

The angle of the bound of a low lob also makes it much more difficult to return than a high straight ball. From every point of view then, it is desirable to keep lobbed balls as low as is safe, and for this reason as much forward motion as possible should be put into the swing of the racket. If a purely upward swing is used for the lob, it will be difficult to avoid raising the ball unnecessarily high in the air, even when the low lob is very much to be desired.

For the backhand lob, the same general rules hold good as for the backhand drive. The body should be turned around so that the playing shoulder is toward the net and the feet are lined up almost in the direction that the ball is to be sent. As the upward swing of the racket requires it to start very low in the forward swing, the body should be bent somewhat away from the net; the left knee bends a little to let the shoulder drop.

With the racket turned slightly backward in the grip, as in the forehand lob, and the thumb extended behind its handle for support, the stroke is inclined to be even a little more upward in direction than the forehand lob. The ball should be met further forward than on the other side, and this makes it more difficult to swing as straight and still lift the ball as in the other stroke.

The finish of the stoke in both cases is in an upward direction, and the racket should be allowed to follow after the ball as long as possible. The body swing cannot be pronounced, as the forward motion is not long enough. The elbow should be bent more than in the groundstrokes, but the ball must be kept well clear of the body.

Even after a lob, it is necessary as in every other stroke of the game to recover position quickly and prepare at once for the next stroke no matter what it may be. It is as dangerous to stand and watch a lobbed ball sail through the air as it is to watch a drive until the opponent has returned it. In either case, you are very likely to be caught out of position and not ready for the next stroke.

Many a lob that was started with good intentions of being kept out of the antagonist's reach is ultimately smashed hard in return. Except for very low lobs that are well timed and well placed so as to catch the opponent so close to the net that he is unable to back away fast enough to volley them, the chances are very strong that any lobbed ball will be returned and will come back fast.

The stroke itself is of necessity slow enough to allow the other man in most cases time to reach it, and it only depends on how deep the lob has been placed whether it will be smashed or returned only moderately hard. In either case it behooves the lobber to hurry to his best defensive position immediately after every lob has been sent up.

A short lob is like throwing the point away, but what constitutes a short lob is not quite so easy to state. Against the average player, any ball that will fall inside the service line should be considered a short lob, and most players will have long odds in favour of their being able to kill the ball, if they can smash from within 15 feet of the net. Some players are able to kill even from back of the service line, or at least to smash hard enough he gets better length than this.

To be out of danger, safe from hard smashing, a lob should not fall more than 10 feet inside the base line of the court. Except when the opponent is caught "anchored" at the net and passed overhead with a low lob, any lobbed ball is defensive and the lobber can hardly expect to win, except through an error by his opponent, until he is able to turn the attack against him.

A deep lob will often drive the other man back far enough to open his court for a drive on the next play, and the lob therefore will often turn the attack against a volleyer unless he is very quick at recovering his position at the net again after each smash.

The lob is best used as a surprise stroke against a volleyer. To lob repeatedly to your antagonist often means that he will soon become used to the stroke and, preparing himself in position and swing, will shortly be able to smash successfully. If he is given lobs only occasionally, he will be less likely to handle them well and they are more likely to be successful.

When the server runs in constantly to the net and takes a position very close up to volley, it is often a good plan to lob regularly to dislodge him; and such a campaign will often break up his net attack, so that he is forced go give it up. When he does stop running in, however, that should be the signal to stop lobbing at once and go to driving at his feet.

Placing a lob generally increases its attacking power, and the backhand corner near the base line is almost invariably the best spot to aim for. It is doubly difficult to smash lobs over the backhand shoulder, so a lobbing attack in the backhand corner is always the hardest to meet.

The success of any lob, of course, does not depend on speed or hitting power but rather on the touch and feel of the racket in the lift of the ball. It should be so finely judged that it just misses the head of your opponent's racket when he jumps up to intercept it. Insufficient height and distance render lobs ineffective. It is usually better to make the highest point of the ball loop closer to the net than to you (the lobber). Disguise the position of the racket almost to the moment of impact so that your opponent will not suspect the nature of the stroke. This deception is of the utmost importance, particularly when using the lob as an offensive weapon. If you betray your opponent will have sufficient time to retreat neat the base line and get ready for a countering return smash.

VOLLEYING

Half-volley

the perfectly timed half-volley is often a defensive, pick-up stroke and gives the impression that the ball meets the court surface and your racket face at the same time. In fact, the racket strings meet the ball just as it begins its upward flight after the bounce. The stroke is a shortened basic drive played from any part of the court, but because it is seldom selected by choice, most players half-volley in no man's land where there is often no alternative. Forehand and backhand versions of the half-volley are shown below. These highlight the importance of getting right down to the bounce, watching the ball and playing the stroke with a short, firm-wristed swing.

Although it is regarded as the most difficult shot to time well, and has even been labelled the lazy man's shot, it does play an important role in both the singles and doubles game. You should practice it on your own and with a partner on a regular basis or your attempts to half-volley in match play will be disastrous.

Improving the stroke

You should take your racket back only a short distance at low level, keeping your racket head up level with your wrist. On both forehand and backhand side, let your knees bend as you turn on to your rear foot. There should be no loop in the forward swing so simply step in on to your front foot getting as low as possible. The racket face must meet the ball opposite your leading hip and open (tilted back from vertical) enough to give the angle of deflection to clear the net. Keep your wrist firm and follow through with a lifting motion, staying with the ball.

Practising on your own

Place two targets inside the baseline, one near each of the corners of the singles court, and also two targets inside the service line each about halfway between the centreline and the sidelines, as shown right. With your basket of balls, go to the other end of the court and start practising both your forehand and backhand half-volleys aiming at the far baseline targets. Firstly on the forehand side of the baseline, then the backhand side, simply turn and drop balls for yourself as you bend and prepare low with a short take-back. Be sure to get down well to the ball and to transfer your weight as you swing the racket forward in a lifting motion. This will improve half-volleying deep down the sidelines and crosscourt with both strokes. With your next basketful of balls take a few steps forwards on each side before starting, so playing your half-volleys from no man's land, again aiming for the far baseline targets. When you feel confident of hitting the far targets, move forwards to your service line and aim your half-volley at the targets that you placed just inside the service line on the other side of the net. Play the ball from both forehand and backhand sides. As you half-volley from nearer the net, you will find that you must shorten your take-back and angle your racket face slightly further back at the hit.

Practising with a partner

On court, practice forehand half-volleying from the baseline against your partner who must volley the ball back to your forehand from the net position. Try to keep a 10-, then 20-shot rally going. After 10 minutes, practice your backhand half-volley for the same period of time, then ask your volleying partner to mix forehand and backhand balls for a further 10 minutes' practice. Switch roles and repeat the routine.

Progress to half-volleying to each other from your respective service lines. If you can keep a rally going in this manner you are on the way to mastering the half-volley. At this stage you can include the half-volley in realistic match-play practice. Adopt the serving position and get your partner to take up a receiving position. Serve to your partner and if he plays a successful return dipping to your feet, half-volley the return as you move into the net. Repeat this sequence for 10 minutes before switching roles with your partner.

The volley (both forehand and backhand) is the stroke used to hit the ball before it bounces. This stroke is employed chiefly when you are playing the net—the primary objective of an attacking player. It is often called a finishing shot because its principal purpose is to win the point and put and end to a rally.

Originally, all strokes in tennis were made after the ball had bounded, and it was not until some years after the game had reached England from its native home in India that the idea of striking the ball in the air, "on the fly" as we used to say in baseball, came into vogue. But it was only a short time after this that the value of the new stroke was well appreciated. The famous Renshaw brother, among the earliest English champions, introduce the volley stroke and revolutionized the early development of the game.

Two distinct advantages are offered by the volley: time and angle of attack. A ball hit in the air, particularly when close in toward the net, offers a much wider range of the antagonist's court for attack than when hit off the ground. In addition to this, much valuable time is gained by using the stroke, since the player on the other side has less time to anticipate the volleyed stroke than one played from the back of the court. This element of time is of far greater importance than is understood by most players. A tennis player forced to one side of his court to make a return requires a certain amount of time to recover a safe position in the centre, from which he can reach any stroke that his adversary may deliver to him. If he is badly hurried, his stroke falters, and he suffers soon from fast breathing, which also hurts his play immediately. To keep an opponent in such a condition is to maintain a constant attack that keeps him on the defensive.

Primarily, then, the volleying position at the net is the best position for attack, and by the volleying position we mean anywhere in front of the service line, for it is next to impossible in fast play to hit a ball off the ground from in front of the service line. Now, two players cannot survive long with both at the net against each other because the closeness of their positions does not afford either time enough to anticipate the other's attack, and one or the other must lose at once. Hence, it is necessary that one of them retire to the back of his court and assume the defensive when his adversary out generals him and gains the coveted net position. But you must not reason from this that it is always safe to make a dash for the net if the other man has not anticipated you. On the contrary, a very dangerous attack can be maintained from the base line, and blindly rushing to the net is as short-sighted as camping indefinitely at the back of the court. There are correct principles which should be learned to show how and when it is safe to take the volleying position.

Horizontal volleying. There are two distinctly different types of volleys with sharply defined lines to identify them. First, there are the volleys of a horizontal ball, one that is coming straight at the player, and generally pretty fast; and second, the volleys of dropping balls, which are most often distinguished as smashes. There are several variations of these two basic types.

The correct horizontal-volleying position is from 6 to 15 feet back of the net, but it also has its own relation to the position of the ball as well. The volleyer should be directly opposite his opponent only if the ball is in the centre of the court. The playing centre is not always the middle of the net, for if the ball is far out to the right in your opponent's territory, your own court will be open to attack on the same side more than on the other, and you should move over a little more in that direction to protect yourself against the next stroke.

Having assumed the right position in court—whether by running up immediately after serving or by gradually working up during a long rally makes no difference—the actual position of the body differs somewhat from that assumed for groundstrokes. The volleyer does not have time to change position from backhand to forehand volleys or vice versa, and he ready at all times to handle either kind of ball. His position at the net therefore must be squared around more, his feet almost parallel with the net.

For the fastest kind of volleying, it is better to have the right foot extended slightly behind the left, but with the legs spread sell apart and the weight carried low to give the player the advantage of an instant start in any direction. Not to keep one foot a little behind the other makes it slower to get started back for a lob, and the opponent can often catch a volleyer napping at the net and win an easy point by lobbing over his head, if the position of his feet does not guard him against such a surprise attack. To anticipate a sharp drive at either side, the volleyer must be ready to jump sidewise on the instant and the racket must be balanced in front of his body, as when waiting for the return of the service. The "splice," of wedge," at the throat should be balanced in the loft hand well out in front and the player will then be ready to shift it to either side without a second's hesitation to meet the ball. Bent knees and the weight carried up on the toes, as in the other strokes, are also essential to quick starting.

When the direction of the oncoming ball is known and the actual stroke starts, the racket is swung out on that side of the body and back with a short, quick swing that is less deliberate and more snappy than that used for the ground-strokes. The backswing is shorter because there is very little follow-through required and less time to make it. The racket is kept nearly horizontal, except when the ball comes higher or lower than the waist, and then, of course, its angle must be accommodated to the height of the ball.

The face of the racket should be bevelled slightly backward to strike a glancing upward blow, but the amount of this angle depends largely on the height of the ball. For a low ball, which is below the level of the net when hit, the racket must be bevelled enough to raise it back over the net, while balls that are met well above the height of the net require little or none of this cut, for the racket can meet them almost square. In other words, high volleys are hit downward; low volleys, which are to be hit up and over the net, are approached with an open racket face so that the underpin will carry the ball upward. The knees are slightly flexed on high volleys; the knees are bent deeply on low ones. High and low volleys are both hit in front of the body with the feet comfortably apart. The racket head should never point downward; instead the volleyer gets down to the ball.

The stroke itself if much shorter and sharper than a groundstroke. There is less swing, both for ward and backward, and there is less follow-through. The short swing is more like a sweep than a blow, but the racket follows only a short distance, being quickly swung back into line and recovered in the former position for waiting, balanced in front of the player. The body should be swung forward slightly as the blow is struck, but the squared position makes it impossible to follow far after the ball without losing the balance. That is, the ball is merely pushed or punched, and the racket head is brought back with the elbow slightly bent and the wrist cocked. The racket head, both in the movement back and in the shot itself, should never be permitted to fall below the wrist, and the wrist should remain firm or locked throughout the entire stroke.

As a rule you should use the same grips for the forehand and backhand volleys as you do for the forehand and backhand drives. But efficient changing from the forehand grip to backhand and vice versa can be acquired only by practice and, when volleying, this change must be quick and automatic. For this reason, many players use the Continental grip—this can be used for either type of shot—because they find that they cannot change their grip from one to the other fast enough. When first starting to volley, however, it is generally best to use the two conventional grips. When you are more experience you can then switch to the grip or grips that best suit your style of volleying. To volley successfully, you need very accurate timing and a strong wrist. If you think that your wrists are weak, choke up on the racket handle a little. While this is not necessary to perform the volley stroke, it may give you confidence when you first start using it.

It is always dangerous, of course, to stand too close to the net, and beginners who find it difficult to get back fast enough to smash lobs will do better to stand 3 or 4 feet back of the position from which they expect to volley, and then step forward to meet the ball when the time comes to make the stroke. Stepping forward like this as you strike increases the power of any volley stroke, as well as acting as a safeguard against overhead attack by a lob.

Always take a volley shot as high as possible and direct the ball downward in order to place your opponent at the greatest possible disadvantage. This can be achieved by opening up the racket face so that the ball will bite the ground quicker and will not bounce up to any degree. The direction of your shot can also be controlled or angled (this is called an *angle volley*) off and away from an opponent by regulating the timing of your stroke. For a straight-down-the-middle shot, the ball should be hit just in front of your forward foot. If you wish the ball to angle to your left, punch it slightly earlier than you would for the shot straight down the court. To push the ball off to your right, time your punch a fraction later or hit the ball a little farther out from your left foot.

As was stated earlier, little follow-through is

needed in making most volley strokes and that which occurs is largely from the action of your wrist. Actually, when volleying close to the net on a hard-hit ball, all that is needed at impact is a tightening of your grip on the racket, letting the racket remain still. The resulting effect is the same as if the ball were to hit a solid wall. But it is very important that the ball strike the centre of your racket so that it will have enough force to carry it back over the net.

When volleying a slow-or medium-speed ball, you can increase the length of your backswing and follow-through. This type of shot is called a *drive volley* and is made for a kill. In the drive volley, the racket head should not go much father back than your right shoulder, but there should be a follow-through to give the shot speed. Contact should be made with an open-face racket, and the ball should be hit down. The wrist may be bent slightly as the racket is drawn back, but it should be firm and locked at impact. The racket should be firm and locked at impact. The racket shoulder should turn toward the net as the ball is punched over, and the extent of the follow-through is controlled by the locked wrist. Remember that the drive-volley shot can be compared with the close-in body punch or jab of a boxer—a compact punch with a great deal of power behind it.

You can control the direction or angle of a backhand volley by the positioning of your left foot and by regulating the point of impact. For a volley shot straight down the court, the point of impact should be well in front of the body. The left foot should be parallel to the net and directly in back of the right. For a volley shot that you wish to angle off to your right, punch at the ball a little earlier than for the straight shot and at the same time the back foot should be brought forward. For a shot to your left, you should punch at the ball a fraction later (closer to your body) and the rear foot, if possible, should be a little farther back. The backhand drive volley is played in the same manner as for the forehand style except that the procedure is reversed.

Special effort should always be made to meet the ball at a point higher than the net whenever possible. A volley becomes more defensive than aggressive when struck from lower down, as in that case the ball must be lifted back over the net, and this robs it of its attacking power. Actually, the low volley, especially one just a few inches above the court, should be employed only when it is impossible to play the ball off the ground (after the bounce). Low volleying is a purely defensive weapon and, unless perfectly played, is rarely effective even as good defence since the stroke all too often results in a pop-up. This, of course, gives your opponent a chance for a kill.

Regarding the placing of volleys, everything depends on the position of the antagonist. First, the volley should always be deep back into the other court, unless a short stroke is certain to end the rally. To let the opponent reach the ball in close to you spells disaster every time, for the volleyer has very little time to prepare for his stroke under the most favourable conditions, and, if the opponent is close to him, this will be so short that he must often miss the stroke from lack of time to swing on the ball even though it comes straight at him.

The unexpected point is always the best attack against the opponent, but, other things being equal, the extreme backhand corner is perhaps the most vulnerable spot. From that position it is most difficult to pass a volleyer at the net, and this offers the most profitable point for attack, as a rule.

But there are other considerations than power of attack. Often a volleyer himself is in trouble and needs defence. He may be hard pressed, jumping from side to side so fast that he is in imminent danger of being passed on the next play. Then the middle of the court is the safest place to direct a volley stroke. From the middle of the court, the opponent will find the angles for passing more difficult than from the sides, and a deep volley down the centre of the court to near his base line is generally a safe return. The ball can be directed best with the swing of the arm, but the wrist also can be bent slightly and deflect the ball to one side or the other at will. Some good players swing the whole body around to place a ball across the court on the volley, but this style generally defeats its own object by showing the opponent which may the ball is going.

Smashing and overhead volleying. The distinction between overhead volleying, or smashing, and the horizontal volley lies chiefly in the angle at which the ball is taken. For these strokes the ball is met higher up and driven downward. With the head of the racket above the arm and shoulder, ready to meet a dropping ball, the stroke is completely altered from that used in horizontal strokes, and even more closely resembles the blow of a woodsman's ax than the service.

There is much more freedom in this position, and

a longer swing and follow-through are permitted. For the smash the player can put all his power in the stroke and hit the ball as hard as he is able. The horizontal volley is apt to be a cramped, punched stroke, while overhead the play is freedom itself.

The smash is primarily a killing stroke. It is intended to end the rally every time, and the player, if he is fairly close to the net, calculates, as a rule, that he will be able to kill the ball with that stroke. He does not expect another return and the smash is therefore played with great abandon. Some players even lose their balance at the end of the stroke and make little or no effort to recover position to be ready for another, in case the unexpected should happen to kill. These are poor tactics, however, and dangerous always.

The smash is a stroke that is properly used only on a lob, for no other return provides the dropping lifeless ball needed for its execution. On a short lob, that is, a ball that falls within 12 to 15 feet of the net, the risk of error is small, and even this risk decreased rapidly as the distance to the net is lessened. When within 10 feet of the net, it is always safe to hit the ball hard, and when so close as this it is seldom difficult to earn a clean ace by smashing the right "through" the other man.

The deeper the ball to be smashed, the more difficult it is to handle; the danger of missing increases very rapidly, and when a lob drops back of the service line, it depends entirely on the individual skill of the player whether it's better to smash than to volley the return. To ease up on a smash generally results in ruining the stroke. If the full power and speed cannot be risked, it is generally better to change the stroke to a volley and wait for a better opening for the attempt to kill. Making the smash requires the fullest action possible. The racket should start well behind the back with a full backswing and come forward with rapidly increasing energy, striking the ball with a sharp impact. The entire body weight should be thrown into the blow, and there should be a full body swing and follow-through to add to the power of the stroke. No other stroke of the game is played so "wide open," for as this shot is expected to end the rally nine times out of ten, the attitude is one of finality that permits the player literally to throw himself at the ball regardless of what may follow.

The ball should always be met with an "open" racket, that is, with the full face of the stringing exposed, the face being at right angles to the direction of the ball, and it is essential that the ball should be struck in the centre of the strings. Twist is almost unnecessary, although some players have an inclination to wrap the racket around the ball slightly, as in the service, and this has a tendency to keep the ball somewhat better under control.

The position of the player for a smash or an overhead volley is very important. He must be directly under the ball for a smash, and nearly as far forward for the volley. Nothing will ruin an otherwise good smash so quickly as to stand too far back for the ball. As in the service, this positions is almost sure to bring it down into the net instead of over into the adversary's court.

For a hard smash, the player should stand so directly under the ball that, if he should miss it, the ball would fall on his head, but the whole body should be bent somewhat forward so the head would be slightly in front of the rest of the body. For a less severe volley, the ball can be slightly in front of the player's position, but under no circumstances should it be forward enough to make him reach out far for it. This is a fault that is almost certain to bring failure.

One of the most common mistakes of beginners is to try to smash every high ball that they can reach. The smash is a stroke is a stroke that is used far more than is necessary, both because it wastes the player's strength and because it often entails an unnecessary risk. Hosts of overhead balls, even short lobs at the net, can be killed quite as effectually with a well-directed volley as by a smash, and this stroke results in fewer errors.

It is a safe rule to remember, when you have a dropping ball to handle, that it should be smashed only when you feel certain that you will not miss the shot. If the opponent is off to one side of the court, even then it is not necessary, as a sharp volley to the other side will be just as effective and more easily made. If the opponent is close to you, play the ball straight at him fast and he will have little or no chance of returning it, but if he is at the back of his court and ready for a ball in the centre, smash to the edges if you feel sure of the stroke, or volley off to one side. As mentioned earlier, on a deep lob, the smash is almost always dangerous, and a deep volleyed return will generally give you another chance at the ball, with perhaps better chances for success on a shorter return. The player who takes few risks with deep lobs and patiently waits for an easy ball to kill generally wins out in the end, while the dashing swashbuckler who wants to bury every ball in the ground is always found among the losers.

In some cases, the overhead smash can be a groundstroke. That is, it can be executed when a ball bounces high in the air. The mechanics of this smash are the same as the overhead volley smash h just described. The overhead volley of a horizontal ball calls for a full swing, a sharp impact with less twist than any other stroke of the game (unless it be the lob), and a medium follow-through. The success of the shot depends more on direction than on the mere execution of the play. It is an easy stroke to make and not difficult to direct. If the adversary had left an opening, it should afford an ace on the next play, but if he is well covered up and the ball is over the centre of the net, a deep volley into one corner will often open up the way for a clean ace on the next return. This stroke is so simple and affords so many chances to kill that the experienced player seldom offers his opponent such an opening.

Overhead volley strokes are made with much the same motions as the smash, except with less speed or abandon and with more caution to control the ball. That is, you will lessen the backswing, and stop the racket behind the head, hitting with a slower motion. Sometimes a slight bevel on the face of the racket, to overcome the dropping angle of the ball, will lessen the danger of missing from far back in the court. Also the finish differs slightly. With the overhead volley, the racket is stopped out in front of the player, about opposite the waist as a rule, and it is quickly recovered at the finish to a safe position for the next stroke, no matter what may come. For the smash, remember that the racket is allowed to follow after the ball as far as it will go and generally ends close to the ground at the end of the swing.

The lob volley. The lob volley, in which the ball is pushed up over the head of your opponent at the net, is another very useful variant of the volley, especially in doubles. It is not, however, easy to play. It must obviously be made sufficiently high to be sure of being out of your opponent's reach, and at the same time sufficiently fast to make it impossible for him to get back in time to take if off the ground. Otherwise he gets an easy smash.

Since this lob shot is usually played in much the same manner as the low volley shots (both forehand and backhand), all instructions for these strokes apply here. The only major difference is that in the case of the lob volley, the racket face is opened to a greater angle. You still need the same backspin to control the ball but little or no follow-through is necessary. The weight should be on the forward foot at impact.

The stop volley. The stop volley (also called a *drop volley* is another very effective form of the volley. It is a volley stroke, hit either forehand or backhand, in which the ball barely drops over the net. To execute it, you should be right up to the net. Hold your racket upright, and, just as the ball comes to it, move it either upward, with a dragging action, or downward, with a digging action. However fast the ball is coming to you it will drop quietly, very dead, just over the net. Indeed, the harder your opponent's drive, the more effective the stop volley. Fingers and wrist, here again, must be very delicately employed. Actually, the stop volley's aim is to keep the ball away from your opponent. Its success depends on the deftness and delicacy of your touch. At impact, the wrist should be loose and flexible. The purpose is to stop the flight of the oncoming ball and to drop it just over the net with a minimum bounce. While it is a rather simple stroke and is fairly easy to perform, there is considerable danger that the return will either fail to clear the net or go too far over; in the latter case your opponent will return it and either pass or lob you, leaving you standing helpless at the net.

The drop shot. This shot closely resembles the stop volley, but it is a groundstroke. While its execution is much the same, it is very much more difficult to make. It requires greater delicacy of touch than any other stroke in tennis, and the faster the ball approaches the more difficult it is to make. Its success depends on your ability to hit the ball with considerable backspin and just enough forward motion to clear the net.

To accomplish this, the racket is held loosely and its forward motion results from a flick of the wrist. The face of the racket should be opened at an angle of 45 degrees or more from the vertical—the forward part of the rim being the lowest part of the racket face. The racket moves downward as well as forward, the downward motion being about equal to the forward motion. No follow-through is needed. The result of this stroke is a miniature lob with plenty of backspin. Because of the lower bounce, drop shots are much more effective on grass than on a hard or fast court.

A drop shot should be used only when made from a position inside the service line and a stop volley only when practically on top of the net; and in both cases only when your opponent is very deep or so hopelessly out of position that he has no chance whatsoever to retrieve the return. If he can reach and return either shot, you will both be so close to the net that your court will be wide open and the point very likely his. To be most effective, both the stop volley and the drop shot should be disguised to resemble something else. For example, the stop volley should be masked as drive volley, while the drop shot's preparation should be made to resemble that of a forehand or backhand drive.

The half volley. The half volley is, technically. Also a groundstroke, the ball being hit when it has risen only an inch or two from the ground. It is usually a defensive stroke used either when you are caught out of position or against balls that bounce at your feet. As you have so little time in shot to play. The half volley may be hit either forehand or backhand.

The technique of the half-volley stroke (sometimes called a *pickup shot*) is very much the same as that for the low volley; that is, the same grip, same stance, and a short backswing are employed, with short follow-through. Since the ball is played near the ground and very soon after it has bounced, you should bend from the knees and waist to keep the wrist stiff and the racket head from hitting the ground. The ball should not be stroked but should merely be blocked by placing the head of the racket a foot or so behind the point at which you judge it will hit the ground; the momentum of the ball provides the power for the return. While on a few occasions the racket face should be open as in a low volley, the majority of the time the ball should be hit with a closed-face racket.

The closing of the racket face is not a wrist action,

but rather it is a rolling over of the entire arm in the same manner as for the forehand drive. This rolling over is very important since if you do not do it, the ball will sail out of court, while if you just move your wrist, the ball will probably end up in the net. The impact point should be slightly ahead of your forward foot, but often you will be caught without time to place your body correctly. At these times the ball still is met out in front of the body, but to the side. Keep your head down as the racket follows through on its up-and-over course. This will steer the ball where you want it to go.

It is most important consideration in lawn tennis to keep the eye on the ball until it has left the racket and never to make strokes with the body too erect, the follow-through being better accomplished with a slight leaning of the body with the stroke. In the half volley, the follow-through is a quicker process than in ordinary groundstrokes.

THE SERVICE STROKE

The service, as previously mentioned, is the stroke used in putting the ball in play. It is the only stroke in tennis in which the player has complete control over the ball—as well as the only shot made which the ability of your opponent does not affect. Thus, it is a wise player who takes full advantage of his serve. For instance, a good service immediately puts your opponent (the receiver) on the defensive by forcing him out of position or playing to his weakness. This gives you the opportunity to obtain the maximum benefit from the rest of your vice games, you never will lose a set or a match.

There are, however, many varieties of the service stroke, and no two of the best players use *exactly* the same style of delivery. More than any other stroke of the game, the mechanics of this particular play are left almost entirely to the individuality of the player. It opens up a lot of possibilities for this service stroke, to be told simply that you may stand at almost any point you please behind the base line and hit a ball into the opposite court in any way you please, when you please.

You have time to wait and think out your motions before you hit the ball, and your originality has much more chance for play here than in the heat of battle where the action is much faster, with less time to think of the stroke. It is very evident that many players have put their minds on this problem, with varying results that have developed many kinds of deliveries. But in spite of this fact, there are three principal types of service: the slice; the American twist; and the flat serve, or cannonball. All three follow the same basic techniques of grip, stance, and delivery, but vary in how the racket head strokes the ball and in the follow-through. The service stroke itself is usually a long, free, rhythmic swing in a continuous motion. It is similar, to a degree, to that of the overhead volley stroke. Like the other strokes of tennis, the service requisites are good footwork, smooth body action, and correct method of hitting the ball. All of the very good servers follow closely the same set of fundamentals.

The grip. The grip for the service is again a matter of individual preference. Most experts, however, seem to prefer the Continental grip. But, for the beginner it is usually best to use the same grip that he uses for the forehand drive stroke. After he has learned to make his toss and delivery correctly, and has gotten his timing, he can try the Continental serving grip.

The major difference between the modified Continental serving grip and the basic Continental is that the fingers are spread out more, the forefinger extending up the handle like a trigger finger. This permits more flexibility of the wrist, which is necessary to impart the various spins employed in serving.

The stance. In taking the proper readiness position for the service, the left foot should be forward and about 3 to 6 inches behind the base line. The angle of the left foot depends on the individual. Most professional tennis instructors believe that the best form is to place the toe so that a slight pivot in serving will bring the foot around to a position perpendicular to the net. The right foot should be 12 to 18 inches behind the left, depending on the height of the player, and approximately parallel to the base line. In this position, an imaginary line drawn across the toes of both feet should point in the direction the ball will travel; thus, for serving into the opponent's right service into the left court. To complete the readiness position for a serve, hold the racket out toward the net so that your wrist is at approximately chest level and the racket head is about level with the face. The left hand should hold the balls. Be sure that the stance is comfortable and the body is as relaxed as possible is a position that is sideways to the net. The left shoulder should be directed toward the court into which the service is to be made. The weight is evenly distributed on the toes at the beginning of the stroke. As the toss is made and the backswing started, the weight falls back on the right foot. The forward swing brings all the weight rhythmically into the ball and onto the toes of the left foot. This is exactly the same procedure that a pitcher goes through in throwing a baseball. The serve is a combined arm and body swing.

When serving, remember that you play the first point from the right of the centre mark and serve the ball diagonally across the court to your left into the opponent's right service court. The next point is served from the left of the centre mark into your opponent's left service court, and then alternately right and left until the game is finished. While the tennis rules say that you can stand anywhere between the centre mark and side line, the base of all good servers is near the centre mark. The server who stands at a distance from the centre mark leaves too much of the court open into which the opponent can place the return of the service.

It is very important for a beginner to avoid the error of foot-faulting. The player must keep the left foot behind the base line. He must not swing his right foot over the line before he hits the ball. Many fine players have had great trouble breaking themselves of the foot-fault habit. A serve illegally delivered is just as much a fault according to the rules as a ball hit outside the service court. The causes of foot-faulting are much easier to correct at the time the serve is being learned than afterward.

The ball toss. To serve, the ball is tossed into the air and hit. But throwing the ball consistently in the same place and at the same height requires practice and, to make it even more difficult, you have to swing your racket at the same time. The ball is held in the fleshy parts of the fingers. It is customary to hold two balls—

the second ready for use if the first service is a fault or a let. (Some players even hold three balls.) This second ball should be held between the ring and little fingers and the lower fleshy part of the thumb. The other ball is held between the first two fingers and the thumb.

The ball should be released by opening the first two fingers and thumb when the arm is slightly above shoulder height. For better control of the ball, toss with relaxed fingers and thumb, not the palm, and let the hand follow through after it has been released. The upward motion of the arm should have sufficient momentum to send the ball above the right eye, high enough for a comfortable reach with a fully extended arm, and enough to enable you to hit it as it starts to drop. To establish that height for yourself, hold the racket straight up above your shoulder with your arm bent at the elbow only enough to be comfortable. Now, toss one ball up just to the top of the racket, so that, if allowed to fall to the ground, it hits just it is much better to toss the ball too high and be able to hit it as it falls, than to toss it too low and hit it with the edge of the racket or miss it altogether.

Practice the toss for both proper height and direction for a while without hitting the ball. To check the toss direction, place the racket on the ground directly in front of the left toot. Then as you toss the ball to the proper hitting height, let it drop to see if it drops directly on the face of the racket on the ground. Many beginners toss the ball either too far behind them or too far toward the net. In order to reach a ball in the latter case without falling forward, the player swings his leg around and the foot passes over the base line before impact. When the ball is too far behind, the smooth rhythm so necessary in a serve cannot be obtained, resulting in a poor stroke. Remember that if you do not hind your toss is straight to the point where you want it, you do not have to hit the ball. You can allow it to fall, catch it, and start your toss again.

The swing. You should start your toss and backswing at the same time. To accomplish this easily, the two hands should be close together at the start in a position in front of the waist. As the left hand goes up, the right takes the racket down and backward to a point where the arm is completely extended. After the racket has reached this low ebb, it is brought up with increasing momentum to perform a loop behind the head. From this loop the forward swing is made and the ball is hit. That is, from the serving readiness position, swing the left arm downward against the left thigh and, at the same time, draw the right arm down so that the racket head swings close to the body, past the right knee, over the shoe tops, and then backward away from the net. As it passes the right leg, the wrist will turn outward naturally, turning the racket over completely. (You can feel the natural turn outward in the bones of your forearm). Also as the racket passes the right foot, transfer the weight to the rear (right) foot and raise the heel of the front (left) foot, keeping the toes of the front foot on the ground and the knee slightly bent.

The racket should continue to move backward and upward in a circular are until its head is about shoulder high, behind you, and pointing away from the net. It is now that the elbow should be bent in almost a 45-degree angle, dropping the racket behind the shoulders in an almost back-scratching position. In this cocked position, keep the elbow, forearm, and both shoulders in direct line with one another. This is the point in your swing that you release the ball upward. Remember that the important error to avoid in making the backswing is that of pausing during the procedure. The long swing is necessary to get the weight properly into the ball. Any break in the rhythm of the stroke defeats this purpose.

The upward movement of the left arm starts as the racket head passes the shoe tops. Be sure that the release is smooth—not a jerky pitch—and as the ball leaves the fingers, watch its upward flight very closely. While the ball is travelling upward and after the racket has made a small looping swing behind the back, the wrist and elbow are snapped upward into a fully extended position overhead with the wrist, arm, and racket in line as one long lever. The ball should be overhead and slightly toward the net side of the forward foot. The ball should be hit at arms length above the head, so that even in the case of a short player, it can be brought down into the service court. At the moment of impact, the top of the racket should be closed to the net than the lower edge or throat. The degree of this angle depends on the individual player. Obviously a very tall man would probably strike the ball with a more pronounced tilt to his racket than a short one. The player must use his own sense of touch. If the majority of his serves tend to find the net, the angle is too abrupt. If the serves tend to have too much length, the reverse holds true.

Actually, beginners often strike the ball in front of the head or off to the side at a height opposite the case, but it is not possible to make a really good service without a higher position to strike from. Hitting too far forward will cause the ball to go into the net, as a rule, while a ball that is hit too far back will more often go out of court by travelling too far over the net.

The forward swing of the racket that makes the actual stroke must be started before the ball reaches the point at which you have calculated to hit it. The wrist begins the movement, starting the racket directly upward, and the elbow next straightens out its bend so that the arm and handle are extended to their full reach by the time the racket approaches the ball. Then the body and shoulder take up the work and the full force of the weight is added to the momentum of the racket so that it is travelling at top speed when the ball is met. Everything depends on great momentum in the racket in order to secure speed in the stroke. But the ball must not be met squarely with the racket, as many beginners are inclined to believe. The overhead service stroke is even more of a glancing blow than the drive groundstrokes. The face of the racket should be turned in the hand so that the racket passes outside of the ball, the right edge of the frame, as it appears up in the air, being forward and the other side bevelling sharply backward.

As the racket leaves the ball, all the weight of the server's body and all the power of his shoulders are brought to play, so that the ball gains great momentum from the stroke. The speed of the racket pulls the player ahead rapidly, and before the racket can be checked, he is generally forced to take a step forward, even if he does not start at once to run in to the net to volley the next return of the antagonist.

The end of the racket's swing should be far out in front of the left foot and slightly to the right of it—more or less to the right according to the amount of side motion the racket carried to give the ball the spinning motion. The racket should be allowed to swing forward until it nearly touches the ground, and it is a service to attempt to check the swing at a point much higher than this.

The follow-through is as important in the service as in the groundstrokes, and it is with both shoulders and body weight in this last end of the swing that it is most useful. Without the necessary following of the racket, the ball loses both power and speed, and it also becomes more difficult to control its direction accurately.

The feet and legs play a very important function in the swing. The legs maintain your balance while the weight is being shifted first to the back foot and then to the front. The forward thrust of your body will cause your front heel to rise from the ground during the forward swing, and the right foot, once the ball has been struck, should follow it across the base line. Failure to move the right foot into the court during the follow-through handicaps you in recovering your balance in case of a quick return of your service. Also allow the back foot to follow across the base line and into the court so that you can assume the anticipatory position from which you are ready to begin the next stroke. But, when moving your feet, be careful you do not foot-fault.

The swing of a serve should be a long, free, continuous rhythmic motion. Racket arm, ball arm, and body must all be carefully synchronized so that there are no stops or hitches in your swing. Power in the serve comes from your body, your arm, and your wrist—it is the only tennis stroke that employs wrist snap.

The slice service. The differences between the three major types of services—slice, flat, and twist—are the way the racket meets the ball to impact and the method of follow-through. The slice service is the simplest to learn and execute and the one that should first be mastered. The ball is tossed slightly to the right of the head and shoulder, and the racket is brought around the outside of the ball and slightly to aid the swing in imparting the side spin that adds control and from which the service takes its name. The swing is down and across the body to the left, completing the act of applying the spin to the ball. That is, the racket passes over the upper right-hand surface of the ball as the ball is hit down upon in a right-to-left twist of the racket. The racket must be whipped into the ball with a sharp wrist snap and smooth follow-through. This type of service causes the ball to spin in a sideways direction when it leaves the racket. The sideways spin on the ball makes it curve to the left during its flight in much the same manner as a ball curves in when a pitcher throws it.

In hitting the slice service you rotate the racket slightly during the swing so that its frame is inclined diagonally toward the right side line. This permits your racket strings to hit the ball a glancing blow, cutting across from left to right to get a slight slice that causes the ball to curve downward in its flight. Let the racket follow through down across your body to the left.

The slice service is the easiest to learn and control and can be accomplished with the least effort, and most women and beginners use it because it is not too tiring and the ball has plenty of action. When properly controlled, the curve of the sliced ball is downward over the net and to the left, away from the receiver's forehand. This means that your opponent cannot attack or hit an aggressive return of your service. If the spin is too great, of course, the ball will curve out of the service court. But this can be easily compensated for by aiming as far to the right as necessary to adjust for the curve of your service. It does not require too much practice to determine how much curve you actually are getting on your service, and from that point all that is necessary is for you to control it by proper placement.

The flat service. The flat, or cannonball, service is a powerhouse delivery ad is the one in which the ball blasts down into the receiver's court in an almost straight line. When properly placed, it is very difficult for the receiver to handle. But this serve is a very risky one to employ since it must cleat the net cord by at most a few inches or it will land out of court. The margin of safety is very small. Therefore it should only be used occasionally on the first ball and then only by players of well above average height. Actually, the cannonball should be used as a mixer and sparingly. Let the sudden and unexpected blast of this flat serve be employed to catch your opponent off guard and perhaps worry him somewhat. But for most players, this serve is not a percentage shot, which means if you employ it too often you are going to lose your service somewhere along the line.

The flat service is much like the slice service

except that the toss is more to the left, but still a bit to the right of the head, and the flat face of the racket is exposed to the ball, as the name of the service implies, rather than a bevelled racket face as in the slice or twist service. The follow-through is to the left of the body, about the same as the slice service. This service should be used as a first service only and, if missed, followed by the safer slice or twist service for a second ball.

The twist service. The American twist service is the most difficult of all serves to learn, and is probably the toughest and most physically demanding shot in tennis. It definitely is not a service recommended for most women. But, once learned, the twist is a good change of pace since the ball curves to the server's left and bounces toward the receiver's backward, or away form the direction in which it was curving. The flight of the ball describes a comparatively high arc, allowing the sever ample time in which to get set for the return or to reach the net if he desires. This service is usually played to an opponent's backhand, and it is difficult to return effectively because of the excessive spin and the high bounce. This is accomplished by moving the racket upward and across the ball, imparting spin to it, which causes it to bounce high when it lands in the service court.

The American twist service is started the same as the other services, with the weight on the back foot and the body sideways to the net. In tossing the ball, the body is turned more decidedly until the back is almost turned to the net, the feet remaining in position. The ball is tossed slightly father back and to the left. The weight is handled very much the same as in the other services. It is shifted from the back foot to the front foot. There is a greater arch in the back at the most backward point in the backswing. The racket is whipped up from is low position and comes across the inside and left of the ball, and up, imparting the twist to the shot. As the weight is shifted to the front foot, the racket comes through, starts in its downward notion, and finishes down and, in the case of a righthanded, to the right of the body instead of to the left of the body as in the slice and flat or slice service, as a rule, but carries much more spin. There should be much more wrist action in this service than the others, which aids in imparting the great spin necessary to an effective twist service.

Service strategy. Two services of average speed for first and second delivery are much stronger than one terrific "swipe" and a weak "pop" second delivery. The man who keeps a good average fast pace on his first service has to make less shift in his method of hitting for the second and is less likely to double-fault. The practice of the first delivery also helps him to gauge his error and he is able to keep fair speed on the second ball with less danger of a double fault. In short, the extremely fast first ball is so radically different from an easy second delivery that it does not help the player in gauging his second delivery, and he consequently takes no chances playing close to the net or to the court lines, and makes such an easy service that the ball is frequently killed outright, and generally the attack is turned against him on the next stroke.

Now, having acquired a fairly fast overhead, twist delivery that is well under control, and a trifle slower and a trifle higher to be sure of clearing the net, every player should practice both until he is reasonably certain of avoiding the deadly pitfall of double faults. The next point is the control of the direction. This is of the utmost importance, and no style of service should be adopted that does not permit of the most perfect control.

The average player of little experience considers his duty done in serving when the ball is safely delivered into the opponent's court; he does not see the far greater possibilities of attack in placing the service. To be sure, the latitude for placing is small, but there is ample range to outwit the adversary in even the small space allowed, as his time is short in which to shift position to meet the attack.

Before making the delivery, the position of the adversary should be carefully noted, and the position of his arm and racket to see whether hie is anticipating a backhand or a forehand stroke. If you have studies your adversary or are familiar with his play, you may already know his favourite strokes and what his attitudes mean. If he is a better player of forehand than backhand strokes, naturally his weak spot will be on the other side, while the reverse will sometimes be the case. Possibly he will habitually lean in one direction or the other in anticipating the service, to be in position for the stroke he prefers, and this at once should give the signal to place the ball on the opposite side of the court.

When the server is running in to volley, new problems that must be taken into consideration complicate the service. If the receiver is weak on the backhand side, the server should consistently place the service to his backhand side until he finds that it is being anticipated. The receiver may run around the backhand attack to get the ball on his forehand, or he may anticipate this attack by bringing his racket over into position for this return to that he is able to handle it better. Then an occasional service placed to the other extreme edge of the court will bring him back into a normal receiving position again, or possibly win an ace outright by the very unexpectedness of the play.

If the opponent is found to select one direction regularly for his return from a given position, this in itself can be anticipated often with success. For instance, the receiver may cross-court return, leaning a little to that side of the centre of the court at the risk of the unexpected line pass. Or the opposite may be the case and can be anticipated similarly.

The centre theory is perhaps of more value to the server than at any other point of the play. The most difficult problem the sever has to solve is to get to the net safely in order to secure the volleying position. The centre theory is more fully covered later in this section on position play, but so far as it refers to the service, it is the principle of placing the service in the centre of the court (that is, in the corners of the service courts nearest the centre of the whole court) in order to keep the opponent in the centre of his court, directly in front of you as you stand at the middle of the net to volley. This shuts off his chances for fast ball that will pass you must be aimed out of court, and a slow ball will give you more time to reach it.

Adopting this centre theory, which is most valuable in a volleying net attack, the server should always stand very close to the centre of his base line to serve. By shifting a yard to the right or left he can serve into the left or right court and still keep his delivery right down the centre by placing each ball close to the dividing line of his opponent's service courts.

Against a righthanded player, this will bring his backhand presented to the delivery always in the right court and his forehand in the left court. If his backhand is weak, this will make the right court the more productive and the left court always dangerous if his forehand stroke is severe. However, this attack can be varied whenever one finds that on opponent is handling these deliveries in an embarrassing manner. If the left-court service is being pounded with a forehand drive that is too fast to handle, an occasional service far out to the adversary's backhand toward the extreme edge of the court will often catch him by surprise, and if it does not score a clean ace will embarrass his return in consequence so that an easy chance for a kill will result.

Often the backhand weakness of an antagonist will make it advisable to work on the centre theory only in the righthand court where it attacks his backhand, and to place the service far to the edge of the court regularly in the left court. In this case the path of the server in running in must be further to his right to cover the dangerous opening along his right side line, unless the opponent has shown a marked tendency to cross-court his backhand returns.

Always keep an opponent guessing and off balance. For example, the first serve may be to the opponent's backhand and the next to his forehand. By using such a strategy, you will play your opponent's strong stroke often enough to prevent him from covering up his weakness. This makes for larger openings on his weak side and permits possible aces, or shots that he cannot reach.

When placing a serve, generally make your opponent move to meet the ball. Occasionally, however, it may be good strategy to serve directly at him, thus throwing him off balance. When planing to play the point near your base line, place the ball near his side line to pull the opponent out of position, thus opening up his court for the return. Serve a flat, fast service only occasionally, as a surprise ace or to keep your opponent from edging in or over too much.

If planning to rush the net after serving the ball, a good forcing serve, one which will enable the server to get beyond his service line before the ball can be returned, is essential. The best serve of this type is one with plenty of spin, which insures control and retards the ball sufficiently in its flight to enable the server to reach the net quickly with the least effort. Either a slice serve with some topspin or an American twist will permit you to vary your placement, and if you can serve both, your service attack will be greatly strengthened by varying the direction of the break and the height of the bounce. Speaking of the height of the bounce, watch whether your opponent prefers high or low balls. If he handles low-bounding services well, give him a high-bounding American twist serve. If he prefers high-bounding balls, hit a well-placed sliced serve that will bounce low. Do not overdo this strategy and likewise do not rush the net after each serve. Again, keep him guessing.

Regardless of your strategy, serve from the same spot behind the base line. Do not stand close to the centre mark one time, and then near the side line the next. Select one spot on either side of centre mark (one for serving to the left service court and one for the right), and develop your serve from these spots. The best players generally stand pretty close to the centre mark since that puts them in good defensive position for the opponent's return.

The return of the serve

The return of serve is the second most important stroke in tennis; only the serve takes priority. Basically it must have consistency, since you are bound to lose every game in which you receive if 50 percent of your returns are errors. Remember that the receiver of service is heavily handicapped by the rules of the game. He is forced to stand back and await the attack of the server. He is forbidden to volley the ball, and his first return must often be made under the disconcerting conditions of an opponent thundering up to the net behind a twisting service that makes the ball curve in the air and bound crooked. This advantage of the server over his opponent in the opining duel is responsible for the records which show that a very large proportion of all games in tournament tennis are won by the side having service.

In order to offset this advantage and to get the ball into general play so that the receiver may get back on even terms with his adversary, every ingenuity of the player must be brought into play. But at least he has one thing in his favour, for the sever is limited closely in the area that he can use for placing the ball, so the receiver need not move far out of his waiting position in order to reach the ball. For these reasons it is as well, perhaps, to consider the first return as a play in itself and treat it separately from the other groundstrokes of the game.

But every precaution must be used to anticipate the service. Even though the service court is small, it is no easy task to cover all of it, and the striker-out should be keyed up to the highest pitch for instant action. The anticipatory, or readiness, position requires the legs spread well apart, the body bent forward from the hips and carried up on the toes, while the racket should be balanced in front, with the idle hand braced against its "throat" so that it can help start the backswing in any direction that the approaching ball requires.

As the forehand is usually the strongest weapon of offence, it should be slightly favoured by the receiver. In other words, he should stand a little bit to the left of the centre of the service court. This means that the server has a smaller portion of court in which to find his opponent's weakest shot off the ground. It also allows the receiver to run around any slow serves to his backhand, take them on his forehand, and often make a good forcing return.

The distance at which the player stands from the service line to receive depends on several factors. The speed of the service, the amount of spin on the service, the intention of the receiver and the quickness of his reflexes, all have an important bearing on the issue. If the service is of average speed and the ability of the receiver about average, the best position is either on or slightly to either side of the base line.

Against a powerful straight service it is often who to back up slightly. This gives the receiver a little extra time to judge and handle the ball. A service that is sharply angled and carries lots of spin presents a different problem. The ball breaks away from the court and the player. The farther back the receiver stands, the greater amount of court he has to cover. Against this service it is best to stand in closer. If the receiver is keen to take the ball on the rise and make an offensive thrust off each serve, he must also be in closer. Some players prefer to set up a defence against powerful serves by standing in close and blocking the ball back. The reflexes of the individual are his own problem. The individual must experiment in order to estimate the quickness of his own reflexes. When these factors are added together, the receiver usually finds himself anywhere between the base line and a spot 3 or 4 feet in front of it.

Taking the ball on ruse in returning service is a dangerous practice. It is hard to perfect one's timing to master the return of service when there is less time to get properly set. To make matters more difficult, the receiver mist line the ball up so that it is on his direct path to the net, as he is usually forced to advance to the net after such a return, in order to cover his court. He would otherwise be badly out of position. He mist therefore have both a first-class net game and wonderful anticipation to use this style of taking the ball on the rise successfully.

There are several advantages to the procedure, including a certain psychological edge over the server. He fools that he must make harder and better-placed deliveries to maintain the offensive. A net-rushing server, for instance, is constantly hurrying to get in to the net to keep from having to handle shots at his feet.

On the other side of the picture, we find that this policy results in more errors and bad positions on the part of the receiver. Although often giving a player a brilliant attack, it can also result in the exact opposite, making for inconsistency. Most teaching professionals' advice is to take the ball at the top of the bounce until the return is consistent. "Then possibly learn to play it on the rise occasionally—for the psychological effect on the opponent, if for nothing else.

Most players use a safer method of delivery on their second serve. This may tame the form either of less pace or a greater amount of spin. The receiver, therefore, has a better chance to take over the offensive on the easier second serve. If you move in closer, this usually will worry the server a little and enable you to get to the net quicker, should your succeed in making a forcing return.

When the serve is placed well out of the reach of the receiver, he is often forced into some mad scrambling to retrieve it. Some exponents of the game are in favour of a jump or lunge to cover the necessary distance. In most cases, however, it is best to keep both feet on the ground and run or slide and stretch to get the shot. When you lunge or jump, you are apt to destroy your sense of balance.

Actually, when considering the best method of handing a service, it is necessary to examine the matter in two different situations: first, when the server runs up to the net, and second, when he does not. Against the volleyer, who is fast on his feet and well settled in position to handle the first return, the receiver has four plays open to him. He can pass down the line, he can pass across the court, he can lob over the server's head to drive ham back, or he can drive toward the adversary with a low dropping stroke that is kept close to the net or drops soon after crossing it so that it leaves no chance for a killing volley.

The pass down the line is always easier (for a righthanded player) in the right court, where his forehand drive can be brought into play. If the service is directed toward the edge of the court, this stroke will generally offer the best chance, for the cross-court pass is then more difficult and the line more open for attack. For a player with a fine control of the backhand drive, the line pass is also open in the left court when the service comes toward the side.

But when the server works on the centre theory, or, without that plan of action, keeps his service well centred, the line pass is not open for a fast ball, and is more difficult for a slow ball.

From the centre of the court, the dropping ball is often the bast attack against a good smasher to whom it is dangerous to lob. The cross-court shot can be played slow from the centre to either side, but the receiver is always in trouble against a fast server who centres his service and closes the alleys to attack from a pass up the side lines.

Occasionally, a short cross-court pass will be found very useful from the outside edge across in front of the server as he runs up to volley. A return from a wide position allows a sharper angle and more speed because of the greater distance the ball must travel, and while difficult to execute, it is a most valuable attack for occasional use. This shot should not be played often because it will give the server an easy chance to kill if he is able to anticipate it and lean toward the cross-court position to intercept it. Your own position at the side of the court will make it impossible for you to open to him; such a shot must win outright or it won't win at all.

But another side of this stroke is its value as a surprise and to keep the volleyer in the centre of the court. If the cross-court return of service is never used, an experienced server will find it easy to direct his attack to the far edge of your service court and lean toward the same side to intercept your attempts at passing along the side lines. This is when the cross-court shot is most valuable, and one or two successes with this stroke will bring him back to his correct position and give you an even chance once more for the line pass, unless he centres his service.

If you fail to find the necessary opening for any passing shot, a dropping ball down the centre of the court will make the volleyer block the ball upward again over the net, if you succeed in making it low enough and drop quickly enough for the purpose. Your second shot may offer a better chance for a winning pass, and often does. At least it brings the striker back on more nearly even terms with the server if the latter does not make a very aggressive stroke from such a return of his service.

The lob is often a good answer to a difficult service, and varied with passing strokes at the feet of the server it is doubly valuable. To lob regularly to a server is to court destruction, for he will soon be able to anticipate the shot and then only the deepest and straightest dropping balls will not be killed; even they are likely to the volleyed back so deep as to drive you out of court to handle them. But worked occasionally with the other variations, the lobbing return has a tendency to keep the server from coming in close, which opens up his position in turn for the dropping attack. Particularly is this valuable from the extreme left of the left service court, where the backhand is attacked, and the server is running up diagonally to meet the return. A lob diagonally to his backhand corner then will be very difficult for him to reach, and may make him turn and give you the attack.

Lobbing the service is generally better toward the end of a hard match, rather than at the start when the adversary is fresh and strong. When he begins to slow signs of fatigue, particularly if you are stronger than he at the end, a lobbing attack generally produces good result. Perhaps the most dangerous lob of all for the server is one that is made with the same motion used in playing a passing stroke. It is quite possible to swing the arm forward as though to drive the ball, and turn it at the last instant and lob with the face of the racket bevelled back. The server is almost certain to lunge forward, if this stroke is concealed well, in order to volley the next stroke, and he will then be caught off balance for a probable ace.

The server who remains on the base line presents a different problem. The receiver has more of an opportunity to put the ball in play and to bide his time to go to the net. As a general rule, the return should be a deep, well-place shot, usually to the weaker side of the sever. In this way, he may be forced into making a shot which offers a better opportunity for a sally to the net than his service did. Against a base-liner, as well, the returns must be varied; no set program is practical.

The best way to cope with a base-liner is either to attack from the net or draw him in to it. The former practice is usually considered best of most players but it often pays to refrain from becoming overanxious to attack. It is best to rally with your opponent until he makes a shot well inside the base line. The tactics must depend on the soundness of the server in the different departments. Sometimes, in the case of a player whose serve is less severe. It is better to try the forcing shot from the service return, as that is more apt to be an easier shot than would result from a base-line exchange.

Whatever method the receiver uses, he should remember to mix his shots, and confuse and surprise his opponent whenever possible. Make the server run, and by all means take the offensive away from him at every opportunity.

Changing and correcting a stroke

The only time to change a stroke is when it will not do the job. This is not something to be done lightly; no matter how grooved the new stroke becomes, you may lapse back into old habits as soon as the stroke is put under pressure. As a result, you may end up with a new stroke that is even worse than the old one.

The only reasons for altering a grooved stroke are: (1) you cannot be consistent with the old one; (2) you have no control with it; or (3) it lacks power. Since a change must be made, make the change as simple as possible. In the case of groundstrokes, stick with your old grip. Do not throw away a Western forehand just because a group of Continental stylists regard it disparagingly, and do not switch from Continental to Eastern simply because the Eastern is the thing to do.

It is reasonably easy to make a service or volley trip change; it is almost impossible for most players to make a successful forehand groundstroke alteration.

The best way to change a stroke is to understand what you have been doing and why it has prevented you from hitting the ball in court consistently, with control or with power. If you do not understand where your stroke has failed you, the transformation will be that much harder. But if, for example, you can see that you have closed the face of your racket and that therefore too many open it. You do not then need a complete new stroke; you simply concentrate on an exaggerated "open" racket face.

Never change a stroke just because someone says it does not look right. Some of the greatest strokes in the game have been the most unorthodox. No one ever had a less classical backhand volley than Jean Borotra, but no one ever hit it better or harder. Do not change a topspin backhand to an undercut; a pretty but ineffectual shot—unless your ideal is to look good while losing. The criterion for changing a stroke is: lack of consistency, control, or power. Never change a natural sidespin forehand to topspin. You can, if you wish, add a topspin forehand to your repertoire. Never change an awkward but effective stroke so you can acquire underspin as an additional shot to your game. Do not throw all your strokes out the window because they are "different." If they are preventing you from improving, alter them only as necessary.

Take the case of the player who hits the ball with so much wrist action that his timing has to be regularly, the stroke may be eminently satisfactory for him. He should not change it simply because it is wristy. However, if he feels his timing will never be good enough to handle such a stroke with consistency, he can decide to eliminate some of the wrist and to hod the face of the racket on the ball a little longer. His own understanding of the situation makes it that much easier to handle the transformation.

The pro who automatically alters a pupil's strokes simply because he is not conforming to the pro's ideas is performing as action that boosts his own ego but does not necessarily help his pupil. With pupils who are not yet grooved, changes are easy, but with those who have played regularly for one or two years or more, any major alterations are traumatic and should only be made after long and careful deliberation. This is not to say a pro should not make any number of minor changes such as cutting down the backswing or follow-through, teaching better balance, the bending of the knees, a wider stance, or hitting the ball on the top of the bounce, on the rise, or further in front of the body. The major changes on groundstrokes are a different grip, windup, wrist action, and spin. When the position of arm and/or wrist and/or racket with regard to the ball is changed, the transformation must be major.

A player with a weak service or a tendency to double-fault should analyse what he has before throwing away the whole action. The fault may lie in the toss or in poor transference of weight. If the fewest possible changes are made, the player can accomplish them without too much difficulty.

When a service is unsound in every department but the player is grooved in his serving, the changes should be make gradually. One cannot in one hour learn a new toss, transference of weight, windup, hit, and follow-through. At least two things will go wrong every time because with each serve the player must concentrate on five hid old windup, no matter how strange it looks, he may be able to acquire a better serve by making only one or two changes—and there will be less likelihood of the whole action falling apart.

The beginners and the intermediates (and very often the advanced players) do not know that they want in the way of a stroke. Too often a player thinks he would like to "hit hard and look good," but when he starts playing in top tournament level, he wants a lot less and a lot more—he will skip the looks and much of the pace to go for steadiness and control. He finds that points are won on the other fellow's errors, that a classical game can be beaten by an unorthodox one, and that there is more to the game than just strokes.

Whether the new stroke means a complete overhaul of the old one or two adjustments only, the same formula is used in discarding past reflexes and learning new ones. First, the player must understand what he has been doing and more important, what he has been doing and more important, what he is now trying to do. He must be willing to give ample time to the learning process, he must not expect to acquire the new stroke in one day, one week, or one month, and he must never revert back to the old habit. In other words, he must be mentally attuned to the program.

Second, he must learn to perform the stroke (or that segment of the stroke which he is learning) without a ball—i.e., in front of a mirror or, if he has professional help, to the satisfaction of his coach. If he cannot execute the stroke well without a ball, how can he do it well with one? The beginner will work on one phase of the stroke only; the advanced player has a less difficult job, although "unlearning" can be as frustrating as learning.

Third, the player now tests his stroke with a ball, but in the simplest possible manner. If it is a forehand, he learns to play it by dropping a ball and then hitting it or by having a coach or friend "feed" him balls. Once the concept is firmly set in his mind, he can utilize the backboard to best advantage. He practices the stroke itself, with the emphasis, the more confidence he achieves in his new weapon and the less likely he is to revert to the old stroke.

Fifth, when the new stroke appears to "work" against lesser players, he can test it out against a better, more forceful calibre of opposition. But the player must have the right mental outlook; he is practising and learning, and the emphasis should be on hitting the new stroke properly, not on winning.

Sixth, when the new stroke is an integral part of the player's repertoire, the intermediate or advanced player is ready to use it in tournaments. This can take anywhere from 3 months to 6 months, provided the player has been practising regularly and conscientiously. The novice or beginner can also enter tournaments in his own classification; his game is far from polished, but when segments of his stroke are grooved, he also is ready to use them in competition.

3

COURT TACTICS AND STRATEGY

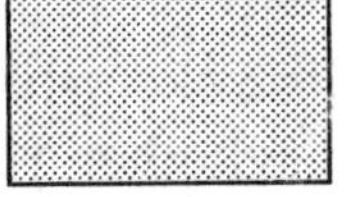

The game of tennis combines skill in execution of the shots with a good deal of thinking on the part of the player. This thinking has to do with where the ball should be hit, how it should be hit, and from what position in the court it should be played. Strokes are not sufficient, by themselves, to produce top-grade tennis. Many players possessing beautiful stroke production are constantly defeated by opponents who are distinctly inferior in this department. To enjoy the most success a player must arrive at a combination of good stroke production and good court tactics.

The subject of court tactics cannot be dismissed with a fixed set of rules and regulations. Instead, the player must consider the different possibilities and organize them as he sees fit. He must use standard strokes, but must vary the depth and pace of his shots in order to enjoy the most success. The game has progressed so much is the last decade that the player must be able to apply these fundamentals from any position in the court. For this reason, the all-court style of play is the only one that completely fills the bill. I would advise the young player to set this as his goal. A game built on base-line play or on net-rushing tactics the other hand, and all-court game keeps the opponent guessing.

Player position and the placement of the ball

The very foundation of court tactics is to play a purposeful game. You should determine before each stroke whether you are going to try to win a point, or whether you are merely keeping the ball in play and returning a defensive stroke so as to get yourself in better position. Purposeless tennis is the cause of much grief. The player should not strive for a forcing shot or winner on every return. As a matter of face, he should not strive for this unless and until he is able satisfactorily to get himself into position to reasonably expect a placement, or unless he is striving to pull opponent out of position for a point shot later.

Perhaps the most important theory of purposeful position play was first laid down by Wilfred Balleley of England in the book which he wrote on the game in the 1890s, when he and his brother were at the height of their fame. This is: The part of the court which lies between the base line and the service line is "forbidden territory." You ought never to come to rest in it; it should only be used as a means either of getting up to the net from the base line, or of getting back behind the base line from the net. If you take up four position, either for attack of defence, in the "forbidden territory," it is long odds that you will lose the ace against an opponent of equal stroke-playing capability. Your opponent will either drive hard at your feet—the most difficult stroke of all to return—or, more probably, drive right past you so deep that you will be unable to get back in time to reach the ball; and even if you do, you will be trying to return it over a net from which you are running away—and almost hopeless endeavour. Against a better player you are never likely to win an ace at all in that position. Do not stop there. There are two purposeful places from which you should conduct your campaign. One is the volleying position—the position of attack—for which you should always be between the net and the service line, and as near the net as you can get. The other is the groundstroke position—the position of defence—for which you should be drawn into the "forbidden territory" to make a stroke, leave it instantly the stroke is made, to regain or recognize that you must act on the defensive.

After the service has been delivered, the server may run in to volley the next return of his opponent, or he may stay back and wait to play it after the bound. The latter method is much the better until a considerable degree of skill has been gained. If one runs in, he must be prepared to jump very quickly to the right or the left to intercept a wide return, and he must be able to hit on the run, for there will be not time when volleying at the net to get set foe the stroke or to deliberate long on which stroke to play.

But whether you decide to run in or stay back, remember the "forbidden territory" rule just given: Go all the way in or stay all the way back. Do not hesitate halfway in the matter, for nothing is more deadly than to be caught part of the way up toward the net and meet the ball at your feet. This general rule applies to all strokes in the game. After each stroke that you have made, either stay back at the base line or run all the way in to within 10 or 15 feet of the net. Against an opponent who drives a swift ball, it is better to stay well behind the base line in awaiting the next return, for you can get better force in your stroke if you are moving forward to meet the ball when you hit it than if you stand still or move backward.

Expert players often stand 10 feet outside the court at the back awaiting the fast drives of their adversaries, and when they do run in to volley, go up to within 6 or 8 feet of the net. To be caught halfway back means that you must volley a dropping ball, which is much more difficult to play than one flying horizontally over the net, and you must also hit it harder and further in your volleyed return.

Sidewise also, one must be very careful not to be caught in the wrong position, as this will offer the adversary a fine opening to place the ball out of your reach with his next stroke. If you have to run over to one side of the court to make a stroke, you should immediately return to the centre (of the base line, not of the whole court itself) to be ready for the next return no matter where it may be placed.

Establish a base of operations in your mind, and after each play return to this central base without waiting to watch the result of your shot. If you hesitate, the delay may prove fatal, and the next return be placed far to the other side before you will have time to recover and reach the ball.

If you are volleying at the net, there is the same necessity to return to the centre of the court near the net and ready for the next volley. If smashing and drawn back for a lob, the instant it has been hit, you must return to the volleying position near the net or retire to the base line for defensive play, else the next ball may be driven at your feet and the point lost. The most difficult returns of all are those that must be made when the ball strides close to the feet.

In any case, one must take into consideration the position of the adversary, for if he has been drawn off far to one side you will be in more danger of being "passed" on that side than the other, and the "playing centre" will be a little away from the actual centre of the court. At the net this is even more important than at the base line, but there too some allowance must be made for the adversary's position when hie is hitting the ball. If the opponent is far off to your right, move a little over toward this side of the court, and vice versa if the is off at your left. This can easily be overdone, however, and tempts the other man to try a short cross-court passing shot that will be a sure winner if it is successful. The sharply angles return is more difficult to reach, and the difficulty is in creased if you are caught standing off at one side of the court, particularly if you happen to be at the same side as the player.

The return of service is almost invariably made from one side or the other of the court, as the server is by law required to serve somewhat diagonally and often does exaggerate this to a sharp angle to draw you out of position. The instant this first stroke has been made, the player should run to the centre of the court to await the next return, and here again the playing position should be planned in advance, either at the back of the court or at the net. There are few chances to take the net position, however, immediately after the first return.

If the server is running up behind his service to

volley the first return, as is sometimes the case, it is dangerous to return far back of the base line, because from the net position it is quite possible for him to play a stop volley, as its bound is almost always low. With the opponent at the net, it is doubly important to keep well up on the toes and ready for an instant start.

You must use good judgment in going to the net; for no matter how good you may be at the volley and smash, your net attack will fail if you give your opponent a setup. If, you example, the drive which you follow in is soft, short, and high-bouncing, you will almost certainly be passed. If you drive a very fast, flat ball or if you start to run in from far behind your base line, you will not be able to get beyond your service line, and you will then give your opponent an excellent opportunity to drive the ball at your feet, forcing you to half-volley or to low-volley. Thus enabling him to pass you on his next return. As a general rule, follow in the return if driving from inside the base line; stay back when driving from behind your base line.

To reach a volleying position quickly and safely, it is generally wise to play a forcing stroke. Do not confuse an ace with a forcing stroke, however. If you get a setup or if your opponent is out of position, drive hard to a corner for an ace. But if he is in position, play a forcing shot: drive deep to the centre of his court with some topspin, not too close to the net cord, and follow in without hesitation. The object here is not to win the point outright, as it would be with a clean ace, but to force the opponent to make a comparatively weak return which can be volleyed or smashed. By driving deep to the centre of his court, the possibility of an opponent driving straight down the side line is eliminated and this forces him, if he drives, to drive within a narrower angle, thus you limit his choice of drives and reduce the amount of unprotected court you must cover. The topspin will sufficiently retard the fling of the ball to enable you to reach the net before the opponent has returned the ball.

If the opponent's drive is short, falling more than several feet within the base line, there is a chance to capture the net behind a forcing stroke. But when his drive lands within a foot or so of the base line, or when driven out of position, so not attempt to go in; for you will have to run too far to get beyond your own service line before your opponent has returned your drive. His deep drive has put you temporarily on the defensive and you should wait for a more favourable opportunity to go in. To attempt to win the point by an ace unless he is out of position is usually also a waste of effort. This is the time for patience, not for a wild, impetuous drive—the time for you to use your head and try to manoeuvre him out of position or force him to make the weak return which will enable you to seize the net on your next return.

As soon as you have returned the opponent's deep drive, hurry into the anticipatory position for your next shot. Do not wait to see where your return will land; do not stand still, assuming that you will make an ace or that your opponent will make an error. You should know where your opponent will logically play his shot and get in position to return that shot; at the same time keep in mind that he may play an illogical shot to an unexpected spot to catch you off guard.

If your opponent has hit a good shot or you have

made an error in judgment and are off balance, try to make your return as deep as possible, but be sure to get that ball back into your opponent's court. If your opponent stays on the base line, do above the net, and as deep as you can without making an error. He will not often force you after a deep return that has a high bounce. On the contrary, his return is likely to lose its sting or even become weak, permitting you to take the offensive.

Remember that it is necessary to anticipate in tennis. It is a bad move to wait until the ball has already covered a certain part of its trajectory before going to meet it. In such an event you must run faster or hurry your stroke, which results in loss of breath, increased fatigue, and greater opportunity for errors. Certain players never give the impression of running on the court, yet they are always in the right position. Others are constantly on the move, always darting at full speed, and re easily played out. The former know how to anticipate.

Anticipation demands a certain mental alertness and an instinctive understanding of the game. One must not start until the ball leaves the opponent's racket. To start exactly at that moment, the mend must have made its decision in advance, one must already have an idea where the shot will land. Thus one gains a fraction of a second, and all these fractions added together at the end of a match represent the extent of time during which you have set the cadence of the play.

One must not start too soon, for this would allow your stratagem to be discovered and turned against you. Neither must you start too late. The interval is very short—it is between the moment when the opponent is sufficiently set so as no longer to be able to change the stroke and the moment when the ball is hit.

It goes without saying that from the moment when anticipation becomes a natural part of your game, you must take account of it in your method of placing the ball. Left us call the "closed side" of the court that part to which the previous shot has drawn the opponent, that is to say, where he tends to stay momentarily, and the "open side" that part of the court which is least well protected. The most elementary tactic will lead you to play always toward the open side so as to put the opponent out of position in the easiest possible way. When you play twice in succession to the same side, that is, to the closed side on the second shot, you have attempted a deception. Between two players of equal strength and whose strokes have an equal speed, the side to aim for becomes a sort of game of "odd or even." The better psychologist ought to win.

The study of anticipation and deception includes a second step, false anticipation. A pretended start in one direction naturally incites the opponent to try a deceptive shot to the opposite side—which fails because the start was a false one.

There are two ways of making a deceptive shot, in depth or width. It is an error to believe that this tactic can only be applied on shots placed to right and left. A deceptive lob, over an opponent rushing for the net, is one of the most effective shots. Again, a very short drop shot to surprise a player retreating toward the base line almost always wins the point. For a deception attempted laterally it is a good thing to play short, shorter if possible than the first ball. A short cross-court shot is very effective, especially if it is deceptive. It will be noticed that the more one imposes one's game on an opponent's means of reply and one's own problems are less complex.

To repeat, your position in the court must be governed chiefly by the position of the ball first, then by the position of the opponent, and finally by the known characteristics of his play. If your return has carried the ball far over to the right of the other man's court, your waiting position must be correspondingly to your own left to anticipate his next shot. Similarly, you must lean toward your own right when you have played the ball far out to the left side of your opponent's court.

The "centre theory." Speaking generally, you as safer on sharp cross-court angles the farther you are from the net, and the more in danger the nearer you approach the net. Conversely, you are more or less safe in the net position according to how near the centre of your opponent's court the ball is placed when he is ready to make his next return. This is the basis of what is known as the "centre theory," and those who study it most closely find it one of the better means of strengthening their net attack. This theory, with or without its name, was used by "expert" players for a great number of years. James Dwight of the United States was one of the first to make it his style of play.

The "centre theory" is this: A volleyer is in a better position to command the court and so maintain his position at the net if he volleys *down the middle of the court rather than to the sides*. If he volleys down the middle, his opponent must be in the middle of his court to return the ball. If his opponent is in the middle, he will have less chance to drive the ball past the volleyer on either side than if he were driving from a corner of his base line. Less chance, because, if driving from either corner, he can drive hard down the side line, for he has the full length of the court to keep his shot in court; but, if he is in the middle of the court, he cannot drive so hard to either side line as he can when driving straight down the side line, because of the danger of the ball going out of court owing to the angle at which it is travelling. Since he cannot drive so hard, the ball travels more slowly, and therefore the volleyer has more time to intercept it. The only hard drive that can be made from the middle of the base line is down the middle of the court; and this drive, however fast, is generally quite easily dealt with by a volleyer in position.

Both in attack and defence the player who has made a study of the "centre theory" has a good pull over one who has not. In defence (in a base-line duel) when you yourself are playing from the base line and your opponent's backhand is not sufficiently weak to make it worthwhile to keep on hammering at it, you should keep the ball down the middle of the court and as deep as possible, because your opponent will find fewer chances of making a winning stroke from the middle of his own base line, or of making a shot that will even drive you so far out of position that he will be safe in running up to the net. But if he does get to the net, remember that the "centre theory" is temporarily useless. You must either lob or try to pass him. In attack, or rather as a means of preparing for attack, it is also most useful; for when you have driven your opponent, let us say, out to the side of hiş court at one corner, a deep drive down the middle will give you a straight instead of a slanting run into the net, at the same time lessening the danger of being passed. Once settled safely at the net, the centre theory is still a splendid defence of your position if you do not get the opportunity at many times when a man is volleying that he can return the ball but cannot kill it, and then the part of wisdom is to keep the other man from passing and wait foe a better opening for the kill you are playing for. Again the centre theory is needed, for the volley that does not kill is better in the centre of the court so that the next return shall not turn the tables against you and put you on the defensive.

Thus, from every viewpoint, the centre theory is a help to defence and a greater help to safety while attacking. For the man who wants to throw all caution to the winds and rip and slash his way through all opposition, perhaps the better course strokes, but this opens him up to even greater dangers than he is hoping to ensnare his antago-nist with, and unless he is very skillful at this style of game, the safer man on the other side of the net is likely to beat him. Remember that the net position enables the skillful volleyer to dominate the court, and thus it is worth some risk to gain that advantage. By going to the net you force your opponent to make errors by the very fact that if he fails to be accurate, he will give you an opportunity to win the point. This mental hazard is of very real value in long, hard match. You must expect to be passed now and then; but do not let an occasional pass discourage you from continuing your attack.

If the other man tries to dislodge you from the net by lobbing, then you must get back quickly to smash, and if your smash is not an outright kill, you must return to the net position instantly. The slightest hesitation or delay after smashing a lob means that it will be too late to get up close again, and the next return will be at your feet. You will be forced to stay back in your court and the adversary may take that opportunity to take the net attack into his own hands.

When lobbing yourself, place your lobs far back. It is better to risk putting the ball out of court than to lob short. That is sure death, and the moral effect of a smashed ace gives the enemy more confidence. If there is any choice, it is better to lob to the backhand corner of the other man's court than to his forehand side. Few players can smash from the backhand side, for the stroke is much easier when made with the ball over the right shoulder. On the left side, the player is generally forced outside of the court to smash, and if he does not kill outright, then his court is wide open for the next return.

The lob is often the best defence against a good net player who gets in close, but it should be varied. If you lob too much, the other man will get used to handling that stroke and soon begin to kill it. On the other hand, watch for the first time he fails to follow up his smash quickly to the net and try to get the next return at his feet before he comes in close enough to volley. That is type turning point and often wins a long rally.

In smashing one of your opponent's lobs, select the part of his court that seems least covered, but if the ball is falling short so your are not far from the net when you hit it, the direction is not so important and sheer speed alone will generally kill. It is sometimes more effective to smash directly at the other man's feet, particularly if he is fairly close to you. He will hardly have time enough to get his racket into position to make a return from a hard smash right at him, and this is sometimes more embarrassing than a hard-hit ball a little way off, as it gives less room in which to swing the racket.

Depth and net clearance. Top players automatically know when depth is important and when it is necessary to hit a ball with a large margin of net clearance. But beginners and intermediates are confused: they try for depth at the wrong times, and they cannot judge the proper moment to aim fro net clearance.

The two subjects must be taken together because one goes with the other. In order to hit a deep ball, one should clear the net by 2 to 8 feet. A ball that whistles past the tape will fall short, whereas a ball with a great deal of net clearance is much more likely to land near the base line. Depth is important when the opponent is on the base line. A short ball (or one that skims the net) gives the opponent the opportunity to make a forcing shot and to take the net position. Therefore all efforts in base-line exchanges should be toward keeping the opponents pinned back. One only hits a short ball (a net skimmer) when the opponent has been worked out of position. A sharply angles short shot can then be a winner. When playing from the base line, there is another consideration other than depth. The idea is to force the opponent, but not to the point where forcing shots become errors, and to prevent he opposition from getting grooved. For this reason, baseline exchanges should clear the net by different margins—by 8 to 10 feet when one is retrieving a very deep ball, and by 2 to 3 feet when one is trying for added pace. Depth is unimportant when the opponent is at net. Now one tries only to keep the ball low, for a high ball to a net player is a setup. The ball should clear the net by the narrow margin of 3 inches to a foot. If the ball is dropping quickly (falling short), the opponent will have to volley up, which is the aim of the defender.

There is a third consideration. Should one try for depth on return of serve against a net-rusher? A few servers come in so fast that they can make their first volley from inside the service line. The return against them should be low and short (a net-skimmer to prevent them from hitting down on volleys and a fast-dropping ball to force them to volley up). However, many big servers take their first volley at a point several feet behind the service line. The ideal riposte is a ball which will land at the server's feet. This means a certain amount of depth, but basically the ball must be dropping fast when it reaches the area immediately behind the service line. A ball with high net clearance (6 to 8 feet) will not drop fast enough, and it is therefore batter to try for 2 feet of clearance. This gives the receiver a safety margin while insuring a reasonably deep return. But whatever you do, do not stick to one pattern, and always avoid a high return to the net player. Skim an occasional one from the base line in a back-court exchange, go for high, looping bouncers at other times which clear the net by 10 feet, and see how your change of pace will break up your opponent's rhythm and make your hard shots seem harder.

Playing on different surfaces

There are many tennis court surfaces, and each and very one of them requires a different technique and strategy. For instance, the man who is trained on clay always has trouble his first year on grass. Clay players develop an accurate base-line game, and power on attack is not important. It is necessary instead to run down the ball, to keep it in court, to lob very high, and to get back into position. This steady, accurate clay-court champion is lost on grass, where the premium is on speed and attack at any cost.

Grass is a game of moving forward, forward, forward. A stab volley is liable to be a winner, whereas on clay the stab volley is almost a sure loser since the player gets passes on the return. One needs only a big serve and volley on grass; the groundstrokes are far less important. Conversely, one need not have a big serve or volley on clay; groundstrokes that have depth, consistency, and accuracy are all-important. Bad grass is the greatest equalizer, for a man with a big serve and stab volley has a chance against the champion who has not only a big serve and volley but good groundstrokes as well. Games follow serve, and with a few bad breaks (rough bounces) against him, the champ is out.

There are numerous synthetic court surfaces being used today. Most of these surfaces are made of acrylic fibres, rubber, or a synthetic plastic grass, and play about as fast as grass. Because of their synthetic nature, they play more consistently than grass, but the speed of the court can be regulated by spraying the courts or shaving the fibres.

The cement player has a wider choice of games. One can become good on cement with an attacking game, but this surface can also develop excellent retrievers. One can be a base-liner or a net-rusher, and one can win with a good serve or beat a big server with one's excellent groundstrokes. Cement is much faster than clay and it has a truer hence than grass, but the ball bounces high, which gives one a chance to retrieve it. The cement player is usually better rounded than the clay or grass devotee; he is more likely to have both good groundstrokes and a good volley, and by realizes the importance of a big serve.

Aggressive cement players make the transition by grass faster than to clay; steady cement players must more quickly to clay. The average cement player is more aggressive than steady since speed plays off and so does a well-founded attack.

Grass is an unusual surface for training. Grass players have real trouble adjusting to clay and a certain amount of difficulty in responding to the both bounces on cement. Grass is not only fast, but a hard ball tends to slither away from the opponent. It is difficult to groove one's strokes on this surface.

Wood is like fast cement. The trouble is that most wood courts are not well lit, and this adds another dimension to the difficulties of learning the surface. A big serve is vital, but one does have chance to get a good swing at the ball because the bounce is true. Scandinavian indoor courts ate excellent because they are well lit. A cement or grass player can adjust to them very quickly. Most professionals with their pupils to hit groundstrokes with their side to the net. As they bit the ball, the front leg is supposed to move into the shot, i.e., toward the net. This always holds line when there is plenty of time to get to a ball and the footing is sure. On clay, composition, or grass, the player moving toward a ball runs several steps less, then slides into the shot. This saves energy for the long matches and means that the player does not have to be in perfect position to hit a ball since he has to slide at the last minute.

The slide when running to the forehand side funds the player hitting with an open stance. If the player is righthanded, he plants his left foot and slides his right foot sideways to meet the ball. If he were to slide his left foot, he would be too twisted in relation to the net to effect a good shoulder turn and powerful shot. Normally the good slides 2 or 3 feet. When our righthanded friend changes direction and goes forward, it is his left foot that slides; the shot usually looks like a classical hard-surface forehand, with the left leg a little more extended than usual. This spreading of the feet when moving forward is very good since the player hits the ball more in front of his body and, consequently, gets more power. The open stance usually results in a more defensive shot than the closed stance unless there is good weight shift at the last minute, since the weight is not being moved from back to front foot unless the shoulder comes through well. Therefore the open-stance forehand is seen more frequently on clay or composition courts than on grass since on the latter surface most players are always moving into net.

There are few if any open-stance backhands that are satisfactory. In other words, a right-handed player cannot slide his left foot to meet a ball on his backhand side. He is them unable to turn his right shoulder because he is facing the net and it has already been turned. When he moves forward, his right foot also slides because he must keep his right shoulder toward the net until he makes contact with the ball and turns it. Because footing is sure on cement and the surface is so hard, players changing to clay or grass are afraid to slide or fall. But sliding on clay or grass is necessary, and falling properly is seldom dangerous on grass. A last-minute flat-out lunge often wins a point. However, such acrobatic action should not be a circus performer rather than a tennis star.

A great, aggressive champion can attack on clay and win; a great defensive champ can parry a grass attack and come out ahead. The real champion is good on all surface. Usually he adjusts his game to the court, attacking more on the fast and defending more on the slow.

Playing the wind

One cannot always play under ideal conditions. Many times the court will be rough, the background glaring, the underfooting wet, the gallery noisy, the backstops too short, the lighting poor, or the wind hazardous. The winner will have the better mental attitude and the better plan, and he will be oblivious to outside distractions. He will welcome the challenge of poor conditions because he knows that he can surmount them better than his opponent. The loser will be distraught; it is one of the facts of tournament tennis that the man who trails is the man who complains, while the winner takes everything in stride. There are three kinds of wind. It can blow against you on one side of the net so that your best shots go short, and with you on the other so that all your lobs sail out. It can blow from one side to the other so that anticipated forehands come into your backhand. Or, hardest of all to master, it can be gusty, sweeping the ball in any direction just as you are set for it. If you look on the wind as a challenge, you have won half the battle. You are fighting an opponent and the elements, but so is he. If you recognize the fact that not only your best shots but his, too, will be only adequate on a windy day, you automatically have the edge. The chances are that his attitude will not be as good as yours.

Topspin is the master wind shot. When the wind is blowing behind you, only topspin will make the ball drop into court. Do not try for depth; try for pace with topspin. This is not only a good base-line weapon when the wind is with you, but it is an ideal passing shot. Use enormous quantities of backspin on your lobs to enable you to lob high and yet keep the ball in court. Slice all your serves to prevent them from sailing. On the other side of the net, you are fighting the wind. Slug a little more than your wont and the ball will still go in. Lob with twice the strength of your usual lob. On this side of the net, you can be a "steady slugger." Overhit your serve; the wind will bring it in.

When the wind is bringing forehands into your body, watch for the wild bounce. Hit every ball wide to the opponent's backhand. Lob only to his backhand. When you hit a forehand cross-court (or a backhand down the line), do not try for too sharp an angle or to hit too close to the line. Reverse the preceding when you change sides on the odd game. Gusty winds are the most difficult to play. Shorten the toss on your serve to prevent the wind from taking the ball away from you. (This, of course, necessitates a speedup in the service stroke.) Watch the ball like a hawk and be light on your feet so that you can play a ball that either moves away from or into you. Be it lets up, revert to your normal game. When it is with you, use topspin; when it is against you, hit out.

TENNIS STRATEGY AND PSYCHOLOGY

Tennis strategy and psychology are closely connected. The psychological element wins or loses as many matches as stroke production. The game between two well-matched opponents becomes similar to a series of chesslike manoeuvres, each player trying to outsmart the other. The ability of one player to excel the other in quickness of combining physical and mental reflexes usually decides the match. The one who can immediately grasp and sense the right play during a rally stands the best chance to win. The element of surprise is of particular advantage; it can do more to break up the opponent's game than any other factor.

The first and obvious rule of good court strategy is: Place the ball where the opponent cannot reach it. The second half of that rule: Be right at the spot to which the opponent directs his return. It stands to reason, however, that if the opponent's game is equal to or better than your own, you can hardly expect to score with every shot. So be patient. Do not try to win a point with every stroke. Bide your time by keeping the ball in play until some hole in his court opens up through which you can drive a scoring ace. Be satisfied to lose at first if such losses point the way to a final win. Often by keeping the ball in play without attempting kills, you can get a little rest when driven hard, can conserve your strength for your own offensive attack and the crucial moments of the battle. When your own offence fails, fall back on a steady defensive campaign and let your opponent make the errors.

Placing shots is the first consideration. Placing the shots is only secondary. Speed under control is an asset but it may prove a boomerang when up against a player who can absorb the pace and use speed to his own ends. Often it pays to soften your own game and make the other fellow manufacture the speed. You have less pace to deal with and he is likely to make more errors. If you use speed continually your are serving your opponent with a steady diet and he soon accustoms himself to it; whereas if you mix your pace, you disturb his stroking. It is confusing to have a ball hit your racket like a thunderbolt at one time and like a feather the next. Remember that you cannot rely alone on either speed or strategy for success. Rather, you must arrive at a combination of both factors.

You must consider what effect you seek. If your opponent is well off court, you can score a placement by hitting the ball with a slight amount of pace. An opponent who maintains good court position can only be dislodged by a more severe shot. A player should mix up the pace and hit no harder than will permit a good margin of safety on all shots. By that it is not meant that you should rely on a minimum amount of speed. You should hit the ball hard enough, but should not sacrifice safety for too much speed.

There are two ways of playing the game—to your

own strength or to your opponent's weakness. If your forehand cross-court is your strength but your opponent's backhand is his weakness, do you hit your forehand cross-court or do you hit is down the line to the weak spot of the opposition? If your game is based on rushing the net after service and your opponent's game is based on superb passing shots, do you continue to attack or do you try to biting your opponent to net where he is least at home? If you like to hit hard from the base line and your opponent dreads only soft, high loops deep to his backhand, do you hit crisply each time or do you lift the ball soft and easy?

The true tennis artist can adjust his game to play his strength when the opportunity rises but to play to the weakness of the opponent as well. But analysing the opponent is a fascinating process. When you know what his weakness is, you may not have the equipment to make use of your knowledge. As an example, you may be a base-liner who hits with reasonable force and accuracy but who does not quite have the power to deal with a steady, fast retriever. You win a number of points but you lose more than 50 percent of the games. You are far too unsure of your volley to attack regularly. Your opponent, on the record, is not as good as your but he beats you. Now here is a good solution: your weakness (which you avoid and never hit) may be superior to his weakness, so try a net attack. Do not serve and come in. Wait for the short ball. Then drive it or chip it or sidespin it on your forehand deep to his backhand and come to net. He will probably hit up and you will actually learn confidence in a volley because the weakness is so apparent.

If he is a lefty, slice every short backhand you get deep down the line, and then close in at net. Again, your confidence in your volley will grow because his return is short. Playing an opponent's weakness will be your best chance to overcome what had heretofore been your weakness. It will also give you greater enjoyment for you will learn to think and improve instead of simply hitting by rote.

Before leaving the subject of playing to an opponent's weakness, here is an important point to remember: do so discriminately. Plans of this nature do not always succeed. The opponent may be adept at covering his weaknesses and cause you an anxious afternoon. Preconceived plans are fine but they should be made quite flexible. Some opponents will hit to certain spots time after time when finding themselves in particular positions in the court. It is wise to study these methods and base your plans on an attempt to take advantage of them when you discover them. For instance, when playing a good base-liner, it is often good strategy to lure him to the net with the intent of passing him for the point, Since he is a base-liner by choice, he probably is weak at the net. To draw him in and away from his favourite base-line position with a shot that has to be played close to the net would be, in this case, a sound tactical move.

Keep in mind that you should· always change a losing game and never change a winning one. However, too many players believe that there are only two strategies—hitting hard or soft-balling. Some of the suggestions below may help you to develop a "thinking" game in which you make the most of your strokes and of your opponent's weaknesses.

If you have been losing in a match in which baseline play has predominated, try coming to net more or pulling in your opponent. Increase your depth or try alternating long with short. See if stepping up the pace will help or if soft, high balls are more effective. Play one side repeatedly to probe for a weakness. Discovery any weakness in your opponent's passing-shot game. If depth does not produce errors, perhaps change of pace will do it or, as an alternative, heavy spins. If you have been losing while playing an attacking game, change your method of attack. Your approach shots may be short, you may be coming in on "nothing" balls, or you may be playing to your opponent's strength. Perhaps there is a forehand weakness in the opponent's passing shots, or he may be susceptible to an attack down the centre. Possibly he is grooved to your approach, so mix them up.

If your opponent has been winning by a successful attack, try lobbing more (to the backhand). If you have been hitting your passing shots hard, try soft, dipping balls. He may have been outguessing you; do not hit cross-courts (or down-the-lines) exclusively. A counterattack may take the play away from him.

If your serve has not been an effective weapon, try hitting it harder or, if your first serve has not been going in, throw in your second serve first. If your opponent has been stepping around your serve to the backhand, try a wide slice to the forehand. If you have stayed back, vary your tactics by coming in. Changing of pace can be as effective on the serve as it is on groundstrokes if you use your head.

It is fairly easy to understand the reason for

changing one's game when losing. The next step is to know at what time the change should take place if it becomes necessary. In three-set matches, the loss of the first set due to a single breakthrough service is no sign that your game may not prevail—stick to it. However, the loss of the first set plus another breakthrough or a lead against you of 3-1 or 4-2 is convincing enough to indicate that your game is a losing one—change. In a five-set match, it requires a bit more time to prove that your tactics may not be the winning ones. Actually, great care should be taken and careful study should be given to this change. In some cases, for instance, like the one mentioned above, when you are down 1 set and trailing 3-1 in the second, it would be foolish to change your game if, let us say, you had based your tactics on steady base-line play to exhaust your opponent in a three-set match, and he was beginning to show the strain of the long rallies imposed upon him. In that case, the 3-1 lead would be offset by the fact that in all probability the opponent could not physically hold the pace that had given him this lead. Be sure the time is at hand to change by a clear concise summary of the effect which your efforts are having upon your opponent's game as well as the score.

Next let us consider the importance of the various sets, games, and points in the course of a match. Many players of ability play each point to the limit from the first to the last of a match, with the idea that a point is a point wherever you can get it.

Nothing could be further from the truth—no two points are of exactly the same value, and the keenest players sense this, doling out their resources, mental and physical, so as to be able to give every effort to those points considered vital to success. This has been known as playing to the score.

First, in regard to sets. In a three-set match every effort should be bent on winning the initial set. The shorter the scheduled course of the match, the more important becomes the advantage of an early and definite lead. Up goes the confidence of the leader, off falls that of his opponent. In a five-set match, many players do not take the loss of the first set too seriously, but attempt to win two of the first three, with the second considered the most important. In games, the seventh game of the set is usually considered the most important, although the fifth to the seventh are always vital. With a lead of 3-1, the player should go all out in an attempt to get to 4-1, which usually means the set. To see the importance of this particular game, the fifth, let us say the server is 3-1 and fails to hold. The opponent needs then only to hold service to be level 3-all. (Another point to consider is the fact that a service break usually means the loss of a two-game lead and not just one.) Following the same reasoning, it can be seen that at 4-2, holding means 5-2, a good lead, while losing results in 4-3. It is true these leads of two games appear large. They are. But it is here that every effort must be bent to hold and add to this lead instead of letting up.

Second, in regard to points. The third point of a game is usually the most important—closely followed in importance by the second. Usually these points spell the difference between 40-0 and 30-15, or between 30-0, a huge allowance, and 15-all. Do not risk too much at 30-0, just because you realize you lead. At 40-0 treat the point in the same manner. If you lose if for 40-15, take more of a chance here, then more carefully at 40-30. Play two of the points carefully to one more risky when holding a lead for the game. Trailing 0-40 or 15-40, take a chance. Coming up to 30-40, do not disregard the effort you have made and play more conservatively before hitting for the winner. Take your chances when you are way down; you will not be any worse off and you may score. On the top, with everything to lose, do not throw it away; await your opening.

When playing a better player, there is always a tendency to "press." Actually, pressing means trying too hard, overhitting, going for the big shots, and, often, playing jerkily. The solution to the problem lies in getting ready more quickly. The better player hits harder and/or deeper and/or attacks more. The lesser player feels his only ripostes are harder returns and outright winners on passing shots. But instead of increasing his pace (which results in more errors) or going for the shots with too little margin, he would do better to prepare more quickly. As soon as the ball leaves his opponent's racket he must make his move; before the ball bounces, his own racket is coming forward for the hit.

The harder the opponent hits, the earlier the windup must be. If one prepares in time and meets the ball in front of the body, one can utilize the opponent's speed. A player who cannot generate his own pace against a soft hitter will find he has "natural pace" if he can meet the ball solidly in front of him against a hard hitter.

The better the opponent, the more closely one must follow the ball. Lapses of concentration are not as dangerous when one is playing a weak opponent who does not force, but one is up against a better player. This is particularly true against the net-rusher; one must look at the ball, not the opponent.

The time to try a new stroke or to increase one's pace or to change one's style is against a lesser player; one must stick with one's own equipment and forget experimentation against a better player. Do not go for "the big winners" when you are losing; use the pace that is natural to you, but prepare earlier. This does not mean you cannot work out a tactical plan, but overhitting should never be part of it.

You cannot compensate for a weakness in your own strokes by "blasting" the ball. If your opponent is murdering your relatively innocuous serve, the riposte is not to try to murder his relatively effective delivery. Neither is it to go for cannonballs on your first serve. You use what you have as effectively as you can; if your serve is relatively weak, you try for accuracy, depth, and spin—not for aces. If your opponent is forcing you on your weak side, you try for consistency, accuracy, and change of pace by preparing early; you do not go for the big winners. One avoids "pressing" by early preparation, intense concentration, and utilizing one's own equipment. One can still lose simply because the opponent is better, but there is a much better chance of getting into the match and of playing one's best if these three precepts are followed. You may still be overpowered, but you will be ready for many more balls and you will be "in" many more points.

It is often foolish to try to outlast an opponent in a marathon duel if the weather is excessively warm, unless the heat particularly favours you. Some players lose energy quickly in the heat, while others thrive on it. One must also consider side winds and back winds when choosing tactics. The ball may travel a considerable distance from its intended line of flight due to a strong wind, and the player must adjust his shots to these conditions of play. A player must try to avoid becoming upset during a match because of bad bounces, decisions, or other adverse conditions.

Exhaustion or excess physical strain is to be avoided whenever possible. It may cause the loss of that particular match or of matches to follow in points to accomplish this end. Another important factor in this connection is to avoid running yourself out on unimportant points. It is easy to tear about the court to make unusual gets, and find yourself winded on the net two or three points to follow.

There are some players who are willing to waste time and points on shots that just will not click on that day. This is a foolish practice. Some other shot should be substituted to gain the necessary result if a favourite continues to fail to come off after a reasonable trial.

You must decide whether to assume the offensive or to content yourself with defensive methods. The latter are sometimes quite effective against an opponent using great speed, with a good percentage of accompanying errors. Try to size up the opponent and find which styles of play are most effective against him. It may be that he is weak against a net attack or a combination of short shots and lobs. Ifs these weaknesses, or others, can be found, force the issue. On the other hand, if he is erratic and has trouble keeping the ball in play, rally with him and give him opportunities to make mistakes. By all means avoid playing the game of your adversary. If he wants speed, slow-ball him. If he wants to bring you into the net, change tactics and make him come in. Base your tactics on the style that upsets and surprises your rival most effectively.

The best for an attacking style is the net position. This saves considerable time, distance, and energy, and is most disconcerting to an opponent. If you are planning to attack, do not hesitate to advance to the net at every opportunity. Another offensive method is to draw opponent to the net in an attempt to pass or lob over him, or run him from the base line with a sharply angled return.

The best method of defence is to exchange shots from the base line to force your opponent into error. It is a safer base because it offers the maximum territory of the opponent's court as a target.

Deception and the element of surprise are also important. They consist of doing the unexpected and hitting the ball to the least obvious place. The opponent who expects a shot in his backhand corner is often the victim of a placement ace when a tantalizing drop shot floats over the net. The best way to worry an adversary is to keep him guessing as to what will come next. There is nothing that will wear the opponent out like making him chase into a far corner for an unexpected drive, or causing him to change his direction can take two forms: (1) concealment of your stroke and the direction you are going to hit the ball; and (2) not letting your opponent know where you are going to be in the court. Disguise the stroke and the direction of the ball as much as possible. Also, by feinting with your body—by leaning to the left or right at the correct moment—it is sometimes possible to draw the shot of the opponent where you want it to come. In other words, create a false opening. The use of deception requires extra practice on your part, but it generally pays dividends.

Do not be afraid to take a chance. If you play all your shots safe, right down the middle of the court, your opponent will have no trouble with you because you are not giving him any. Try placing some of the shots inches from the side line or the base line. Try dropping them a foot over the net. Try fast topspin drives, those high twisting lobs, those sudden rushes to the net. You may lose plenty of points in the process, but practice makes perfect, and you will soon find your shots dropping where you want them. Then you have a good tennis attack. Remember that one of the cardinal rules of all sport is never alter a winning combination. The same is true of tennis. If the tide is against you, you must take chances to gamble for possible victory. In such a case, change your game, change your strokes, pace, and method of attack. But never change a winning game unless you believe your adversary has discovered your plan of attack and has mustered an adequate defence against it.

Match play. The difference between a game with friends and a tournament match is pressure. There is no way to simulate competitive play, and the only way to get tournament experience is simply by entering as many tournaments as possible and learning from your errors. There is not enough tension in practice, and therefore your development as a player will be limited if you cannot compete against others under tournament conditions.

Tension produces fatigue. A player in good condition may get exhausted in the third game of the first set of a tournament match. Top players therefore try to avoid prematch exertions which do not pay off. They may practice hard in the morning or have a hit just before playing, but they do not sit in the sun, do gymnastics, swim, or drive until after the match is over.

Each player is an individual and each will have his own method of training which is best for him. However, none will change their routine just before a tournament. If a player regularly goes to bed at 11:00, he should not suddenly go to bed at 9:00. If he eats lightly before playing, he should not switch to heavy meals when he enters a tournament. The one addition to his routine is salt pills, since players are susceptible to cramps because of match strain.

A good competitor goes into a match with a plan. He does not change it after he loses one point or one game; he does not stick to it if he has been badly beaten in the first set. It is good to be flexible, to play more aggressively on a wet, fast court, to serve short and wide against a receiver who plays too far back, to lob more against a player with a shaky overhead stroke, to play steadily on a slow court but to switch to another tactic if the plan is not succeeding.

The mental attitude of the match player is a function of his own personality. He needs confidence in his own game but respect for his opponent's abilities as well. The unconfident player will tighten on his strokes or will resort to retrieving or overhitting as a desperation measure. The overconfident player expects his opponent to fall over as soon as he steps on the court. The temperament of a player can win or lose for him. If he cannot control his anger when he errors on a big point, the match will slip away from him. Anger against an opponent can be just as hazardous. If one expects misbehaviour or mistakes on the part of the opposition, the crowd, and an occasional linesman, one is only pleasantly surprised if all goes well. The old tournament hand is not upset by stalling or any of the other gambits of gamesmanship whose object is to make him lose control. He takes the calls as they come and he does not fly into a tantrum when a linesman or umpire proves to be fallible. He is too good a competitor to let a partisan crowd get under his skin; he welcomes the opportunity of demonstrating his skill and his poise under the worst of circumstances. However, he sticks to his guns when it is a question of the rules.

Among the "don'ts" of competitive play: Don't listen to advice from well-wishers, don't gulp water on the odd games (sip it), don't worry about lost points, don't run for a ball that is going out (it is the mark of a rabbit), don't think of what you will say to your opponent after you have won, don't count the gallery, don't let extraneous thoughts come into your mind, and don't rush yourself out of the match. Among the "do's": When the nervous strain is great, try deep breathing; when fatigue overwhelms you, stay on your toes; when your strokes fail you, go back to fundamentals; when you are down two sets to one and are playing badly, take the intermission; and when you win or lose the match, be gracious.

Practice. The player who moans and groans the least on the court is the one who is in the best shape for his ability—i.e., the man who practices the most and who practices the most and who gets the most out of his practice. He will have his bad days, but the hours he has spent on the court have shown him how to play when reflexes or strokes are not what they should be. Only a few devotees of the game can spend unlimited time on the courts, but it is not just the number of hours but how they are spent that counts.

To the champion, who at one time spent five hours a day, seven days a week, learning the game, match play is far more important than practice. Two or three tough matches a week are all he needs, and if he is in the finals of each tournament, that is exactly what he will get—three easy early rounds and two or three real tests—until he comes to the major championships, where he can expect at least three or four hard matches. His worry is usually not whether he can get enough tough matches in the season but whether he will get over-tennised before the end of the year.

The lesser tournament player—the one who is nationally ranked but who is generally "out" by the quarterfinals—has a problem that is particular to himself. Why is he losing repeatedly to players ranked above him and how can he improve? Does he lack a tactical plan, is he overhitting, does he have a service weakness, is he too unaggressive, is his return of serve faulty, does he understand the surface? A player of this level must learn self-analysis, since all the good advice in the world will have far less meaning than the discovery of a fault by himself. Once he sees it, he can cure it with diligent, intelligent practice.

The poor tournament player who has the desire but lacks the weapons to achieve victory is the man who must practice the most. His weaknesses are many. He needs no less than two hours a day (often four or five) to reach his goal. He is the reasonably good college player who beats the local talent but whose aims are mush higher. He is the first or second rounder on the grass-court circuit (although often his entry is not accepted). He wants to be a tournament player, but his failings are many. Nine times out of ten this player is not giving tennis enough time and his practice is haphazard. He does not work on the backboard, he does not practice his serve, he does not give it full effort when he plays practice sets, he will only work against certain players, he starts the season too late and he is afraid to enter the lesser tournaments. He will be a loser until all these defects are corrected.

The club or parks player has a much more limited time schedule, but he, too, can make vast improvements by regular workout periods use intelligently. He may have been playing twenty years or more, and if so probably is not looking of sensational victories. The most profitable method for him to improve is not by stroke changes, which are senseless for a grooved player, but by regularity of practice and self-study. Every time he skips a week his game will fluctuate, but he can get his occasional good days without so many bad ones by sticking to a twice-a-weed schedule and by analysing the game through looking, reading, and discussing. Analysis if infinite: Does he fail to lob? Is he taking the ball late? Can he start sooner? Is his first serve going in? Is he watching the ball? Is he drop-shotting enough or too often? etc.

Beginner and intermediate players should be on the court no less than twice a week (more often if they can) and should have professional help as well. Desire and concentration will make every practice session worthwhile and more enjoyable. These two factors will enable players to absorb what the pro is telling them, and the regularity with which they practice will keep them from forgetting the newly acquired nuances of their game. The more hours of concentrated effort they can give to it, the faster they will improve.

Skill in tennis develops more quickly from systematic, meaningful practice than from random hitting. True, you will improve through endless hours of casual rallying and play, but supervised practice under the watchful eye of a good instructor will be far more economical of your time and effort. Regardless of your present level of development, whether you are a beginner, intermediate, or advanced player, and whether you have played continually all winter long or are starting over again after a long layoff, taking lessons from a competent professional is the logical way to proceed. There are many good teachers scattered across the land. A description of the teaching-learning process as conducted by experienced tennis professionals is presented here.

Kinds of lessons. Lessons can be classified as private (individual) or group (more than one person). For a private lesson, the pro works with only one person and the lessons run for a half to one hour. This is the most expensive of all lessons. The fee for group lessons, in which two or more people are taught at the same time, depends on the number in the group. In the case of large groups—twenty or thirty—the fee may be very small. Some pros offer a series of lessons, often ten, for less than the cost of that number of separated lessons.

It is economical for the learner and it permits the pro to plan his teaching in a way that provides full coverage of all essential parts of the game. For these reasons, the nest approach to the problem of learning is to contract for a full series of lessons regardless of whether you prefer group or individual instruction.

When talking with the pro, describe your tennis background and ask what length and spacing of lessons he suggests. He will probably ask some questions also. He will want to know your aim in tennis, how much you intend to practice, and how many lessons you plan to take. He will need to know your level of aspiration and your degree of commitment before he can plan your learning program.

The teacher's methods. Most experienced professional use the *show-and-tell, watch-and-praise* method of teaching. In this plan the pro first demonstrates and describes the action to be learned. He tells you step-by-step what to do and how to do it, and he demonstrates slowly as he explains his moves. He points out the important parts of the stroke that you should work on and he tells you what to notice in his demonstration. He stresses cue words to direct action, and he explains the sequence of moves. Last, he demonstrated the end result, the immediate goal you are working for. He makes a few shots, showing the speed and trajectory he wants you to imitate.

He then lets you try to do what he has demonstrated and described. Probably he will first have you make several "dummy" swings at an imaginary ball: if you cannot make the proper swing at an imaginary ball, you certainly should not expect to make it at a real ball. While you are swinging, he analyses your stroke. If he is a skilled teacher, he will first tell you what you are doing right. He will offer praise and encouragement to help "nail down" these good moves. At the same time he will try to build around them to correct mistakes you are making; he will describe, demonstrate, and possibly even guide you manually through your moves and positions in your swing.

When you swing reasonably well with consistency, he will let you move ahead. He may then take you to "fixed ball" practice in which you swing at a ball suspended on a cord or string. In this practice you will not have to time or judge the flight of a moving ball and so you will be able to focus all your attention on the mechanical act of swinging.

After you get the feel of hitting these stationary balls, you are ready to apply your stroke to a moving ball. For this practice, your pro will toss or hit softly to your, giving you the easiest kinds of balls to hit. He stands close to the net and feeds balls accurately enough to let you concentrate fully on your form; he will practically hit the racket for you. As you improve he will gradually move farther and farther from you and feed you more difficult balls to bit. If, at some points, play becomes too difficult for you—if you become confused and have to struggle to hit—he will realize he moved you too fast. He will take you backwards a step or two to review teaching points or to present new and different ones. Temporary way-stops such as these are often necessary. The pro will always have you hitting at balls appropriate for your level. In this way he hopes to move you along gradually. Eventually you will be able to rally with him from full length at your best speed.

Learning takes time. Do not be alarmed if the corrections suggested by the pro do not feel right immediately. A new grip or a new kind of swing may foot strange for a while. As you work on the changes, they will begin to feel more comfortable. Finally the corrections will have replaced the old faulty habits.

Kinds of practice. Besides acting as a practice partner for you, your pro will tell you what kind of practice to do on your own. He may suggest "dummy" swing drills, possibly in front of a mirror where you can see your form. He may demonstrate how he wants you to practice against a background or a suitable substitute such as your garage door. He may want you to rally across the net with your friends or with someone he provides for that purpose. If so, he will explain the procedure for these.

Most pros consider this separate practice to be essential for learning. Their lessons are merely the starting point from which learning takes place. By demonstration, explanation, and hand guidance, they try to give the learner an understanding of good form. In addition, they provide the learner with some practice under conditions as near perfect as possible. But they all feel that the important task of establishing good habits of form falls to the learner. When it is attained, it is due as much to proper practice away from the pro as it is to practice done directly under his supervision.

Understanding the learning process. If practice is to be efficient, it cannot be done carelessly. Learning to hit a tennis ball is not merely a matter of meaningless repetition until a habit is formed. It is a process of conscious effort by which you try to make changes and corrections. Working under the pro's directions, you try to do as he suggests. But you do not always do it right the first time and so you try again. You attempt to correct mistakes indicated by the pro, changing a part of the swing here or there and noting whether or not the change makes any difference in the end result.

In order to make these changes permanent, you must learn to respond to cues of "feel" resulting from the movement of your hands, your arms, and your legs. In order to arrive at a point where you can respond to these cues of feel without thinking about them—when you can do that, you have learned what it is you are practising—you must first concentrate on and learn to react to other cues, mainly voice cues offered by your pro. The cues, of course, will be carefully selected by him, and will be in keeping with the method of stroking recommended by him. "Point to the top of the fence," for example, could be a valuable guide to you if you continue to turn the racket face over despite the pro's advice to finish with the racket face perpendicular to the ground. Usually the ability to feel the stroke consistently comes only after many repetitions of voice cues by the pro or after manual guidance by him or after the repetition of voice cues by the learner.

You may be able to speed the transition of voice cues to cues of feel by describing to yourself what it is you are trying to do. Even though the pro uses carefully chosen cues, they do not always mean the same thing to all learners. Some of his cues may not have registered with you. Putting the action into your own words often makes certain parts stand out more clearly, and often these parts will be the most important parts for you.

Putting it into your own words also calls attention to the difference between good and bad shots. Try to describe how it feels when you make a good shot or when the pro commends you for good form. Remember the description and carry it feels when you make a bad shot. This emphasizes errors and directs your attention to what should be avoided.

It may also help if you ask the pro to describe how it feels to him when he strokes correctly. Ask about the sequence of his moves. Make him define his terms so you understand exactly what part of the stroke he is referring to. If his explanation sounds too complicated, tell him so and ask for a simpler explanation with emphasis on the parts that confuse you. Repeat the description as you try to imitate his stroke. Do not just look at what he is doing: talk about it.

This sequence of watching the pro demonstrate while he explains, after which you imitate and put the action into your own words, can be summed up to provide a useful guide to learning to play: *see it—hear it, say it—do it*. Follow this sequence in your lessons. In this way, you will be using several senses and you will be responding to several cues. This is the efficient way to learn.

When practising on your own afterward, try not only to duplicate the right motion and movements described by the pro but also to eliminate all unnecessary movements. In other words, keep it simple. Do not confuse yourself by adding fancy flourishes and flashy moves. Concentrate on the essential parts pointed out by the pro. Think about your lessons when you are away from the pro. It may help if you write down what you remember about each lesson immediately afterward. Many pros do this, keeping a file catalogue of each pupil so they can keep track of the work done in each lesson. But putting it down for yourself, in your own words, will help you see your problems and your objectives more clearly. Try to summarize the lesson in a clear and orderly way. If you can do so, the pro has done the job well. But you have practice. There are no shortcuts or magic words, except good, hard practice. If you have learned what and how to practice, your money was well spent.

Doubles play

The game for pairs differs greatly from the singles game that has just been discussed in detail. Not only is the court larger and the number of players doubles, but the tactics are a great deal different. In singles play it is possible to score a great many points from the base line. In doubles, practically all of the scoring is done from the net position. Doubles play also injects another element: teamwork. (Two players make up a team in doubles—both of the same sex or one of each. The latter is called *mixed* doubles.) In fact, the essential basis of good doubles play is good teamwork and complete sympathy between the partners. Two inferior players who "pull well" together will nearly always defeat a pair who are perhaps better individually, but whose play and demeanour are selfish and egotistical. Your aim should be to help your partner in every possible way, giving confidence and encouragement when things are going badly, and keeping a cool and determined head in the hour of victory. Because of your proximity and the fact that you are only two in a team, your mental outlook on the ensuing match inevitably reacts on your partner, and it is up to you to see that it is a helpful, optimistic aspect.

A double fault or a badly missed setup by you at a critical moment may do more harm to your side than the actual losing of one point, because it may quite unsettle your partner, who in his or her turn may also become erratic. A consistently bad return of service is one of the most demoralizing faults from your colleague's point of view that you can have—because however steady he or she may be, the game cannot be won if you repeatedly miss your return. In singles you can make mistakes, go out for winners, try the most impossible shots, and you have only yourself to consider—but in a double your partner must be your first consideration—even as you should be his or hers. To combine well, you must know by instinct or by experience what your partner's movements are likely to be, so that you neither clash not leave part of the court unprotected.

Whether you are pairing up for men's doubles, mixed doubles, or ladies' doubles, you should try to find a partner whose type of game fits in with your own. If you are inclined to be brilliant but erratic in your play, then choose a partner who is steady and imperturbable—one who will have a restraining influence on your impetuousness. But above all choose somebody with whom you can be in complete sympathy on the court—this is the most important point of all, if you are to have a successful and enjoyable career as a doubles pair.

As a general rule the stronger player should take the left court, because he or she is in a better position to take more of the game than when in the right curt—the centre-court balls being on his forehand. Also the even points—the second, fourth, etc., in a game—are more important than the odd—because on them depends the winning or losing of games. Hence the return of service of the player in the left court is of vital importance. Find out as soon as possible in which court you return the service the best, and then always play in it, and persevere with your returns until you bring them up to a very high degree of consistency. If you specialize in one court you should in time become quite expert. You may, of course, have to change your court to fit in with your different partners.

There are two distinct formations in the doubles game, either both up at the net, or one up and one back. (The former is called the *parallel formation,* while the latter is the *echelon formation.*) In these days when nearly everyone can volley, you generally see the former combination in action, and it is certainly more effective and greater fun. Two good volleyers will as a rule beat a "one up and one back" partnership, except where the baseline player is *exceptionally* good.

The objective in doubles, is to get to the net and hold that position successfully. The position should be just as close to the net as possible, with the knowledge that any lob must be covered. This closeness depends on the height of the player in question. The most effective shots against a pair at the net are the low, well-concealed lobs and fast-dropping "loop-drives."

Lobs are used to drive them away, while the drives may force them to volley up and allow you to challenge their position. Good care must be taken to defend against either of there shots when you yourself are in position at the net.

When serving, a slice or twist service enables you to reach the net immediately. The volley and smash permit you to stay there and win the point. Sharply angled volleys and smashes are brought into play because of the extra width of the doubles court and because of your position at the net to the right or left of the half-court line. But when the opponents are serving, a clean passing shot is extremely difficult unless you can manoeuvre them out of position, because each opponent has 9 feet less court to protect than in singles. To win the point capturing the net is usually necessary, and the best way to do that is either to lob or to play a short shot, usually cross-court, directly at your opponent's feet. So important is it for you to steal the net that you are warranted in taking risks in going to the net. Quick thinking, good judgment, and daring are at a premium in forcing the net from your opponents.

Service strategy

In doubles, it is very difficult to break through service. One break may cost the set. In protecting the service, the position of the server's partner is important. He should station himself as far inside the court as possible, allowing himself only outside foot or two of the alley; shots in this space are the exception rather than the rule. (About 6 to 8 feet from the net and about 9 to 12 feet from the doubles side line is usually considered a good netman's position. He should, of course, face the receiver.) Next, he must be in as close as possible, giving himself enough room to be able to cover any lob. This position forces a cross-court return of service beyond the reach of the net player, or a defensive lob which may be dealt with summarily. If your opponents have been able to win points by hitting cross-court placements against the server or have been returning the service at his feet, his partner can eliminate this by standing near the centre of the net on the same half of the court on which the server stands. This defensive shifting of position is called the *Australia formation,* and when employed the receiver cannot make a cross-court return without giving the net man a volley and therefore must play his return down the side line. It is a simple matter for the server to run to the net up through the vacant half of the court, covering the alley as he goes.

Since the server must get to the net as quickly as possible, the most successful service in doubles is the twist or slice with a medium-paced delivery. This should be place to the weakest point in the receiver's game, with sufficient spin and pace to keep him from running around the shot. The server should place special emphasis on getting the first service in the court. By the use of medium pace he is able to control the serve better as well as to have more time to gain the net. However, many good doubles servers believe in throwing in an occasional fast servers believe in throwing in an occasional fast service to give a change of pace. Actually, the serve should be of good length and varied, so that the receiver is kept guessing. The down-the-middle serve, of course, is always a good one in doubles since it will limit the angle at which the receiver can return the ball. When the service is across the court, the server's partner must be prepared for a shot possibly down his alley and should move slightly in that direction.

The purpose of the sever is to get in to volley as high a shot as possible. He should try to avoid having to make low or half-volleys. No matter where he makes the first volley from, he should keep bearing in to the net. The centre theory here works to better advantage. A good first volley down the centre of the court draws one of the opposition, if not both, to that point, and may leave an opening for a placement in either corner. If a lob is put up, the server and partner must deal with it and recover the net position immediately. That is, as you run up to volley the return you will not have much time to think, but must make up your mind in a flash what you are going to do with the ball. Speaking broadly, there are two courses open to you. If the return is a good low dipping drive, which you will have to volley upward, send it back from whence it came because in that quarter it will be fairly safe, the opponent of necessity still being back. If the return is an easy volley, fairly high over the net, then go for a winner, by playing it downward at the opponent at the net, who at such close quarters has very little chance of returning it. The nearer you can get to the net before you have to volley the return, the easier the stroke, and the more chance of winning the point.

If you decide not to come in on your service at all, you must try with your next stroke to make an opening to enable you to join your partner. But always remember that the longer you stay back, the better opportunities you give your opponents for attacking from the net position.

Return-of-service strategy

A team that can return service well can do much to destroy a good doubles combination. A return of serve seldom wins the point outright, but it can set up a less forceful return or it can open up the court to the defenders. Basically, there are three possible returns, speaking directionally—the cross-court to the incoming server, the lob over the backhand of the net man, and the down-the-line in the net man's alley. Of the three returns, the topspin cross-court drive is the safest return and should be used nor frequently than the other tow. The length of this drive should vary according to the movements of the server. Should the server follow up the service, then the return should be a dipping shot, aimed to bounce at his feet, giving a very difficult low volley. Another good return to the oncoming server is a sharply angled ball, low over the net, and toward the alley—this shot if accurately played will often win the point outright. It is far more effective to return a well-placed dipping ball at the advancing server than just to hit hard, because a good volleyer never minds a hard ball if it is high over the net. If, however, the server remains on the base line, then a good length drive, deep into the corner, will give you the opportunity to join your partner at the net and you will have gained the attacking position.

A successful lob is a very difficult stroke to play. It must be a good length, and well disguised, otherwise the opponents will see what your intention is and will have plenty of time to get back and "smash" it. The drive straight down the side line is risky, but if brought to perfection will win many points outright. Even if it is not successful and you lose the point, it is well worth trying because you will have conveyed to your opponent the fact that you are thinking of the shot, and in consequence he will keep in position and allow more cross-court drives to pass unmolested. It should also be used occasionally if one of the opponents is inclined to poach (to take the shots that normally belong to his partner) and to keep him from edging too much over to the centre, to "keep him in his place." If, however, your opponents adopt the so-called Australian formation when they are serving, your cross-court drive must be eliminated, and you must either drive straight down the side line or lob.

A good man in the receiver's court will alternate his returns, but his decisions will be based not one the shots themselves but on the talents of the opposition. Remember, too, that it is most important to keep the ball in play when you return the service. Inexperienced teams waste too many points in trying to drive hard foe a clean ace. A short, low drive is much more important than speed. In fact, a drive with moderate speed is usually more difficult to volley than a fast return. A clean pass off the service is so difficult that your errors will probably more than offset your aces.

Do not allow the opponents' activities at the net to fluster you and put you off your aim. The tendency is to have one eye on the volleyer and one on the ball, and the result is fatal. Watch the ball and concentrate and make up your mind—but not obviously—what you are going to do, and unless the adversary moves before you have hit the ball, he or she will not be in time to intercept a good shot. And if the volleyer does more before you strike the ball, you have only to change your direction and push it quite gently straight down the side line to win the point.

The return of service resolves itself into a battle of wits between the receiver and the opponent at the net—the former trying to avoid the latter, and the latter endeavouring to intercept the drives of the former. It is difficult to define the best position for you to take when your partner is receiving the service, but it generally depends on two things: the movements of the sever and the general quality of your partner's return. When the server remains back you should certainly stand up at the net, because you are in the attacking position. Also, if your partner has a good return of service you should stand close to the net irrespective of what the server is doing, as you may have an opportunity of intercepting the server's return. Only when your partner is having great difficulty with the service, and more often than not putting the ball on to the opponents' rackets, should you stand back, because under these circumstances your position at the net is useless, whereas if you are back you have a chance of picking up the opponents' volleys. If there is any doubt as to which position is better, the simplest thing is to ask your partner's opinion as to where you should stand while this particular service is in progress.

To return service well in doubles, one needs concentration to a superb degree, mental relaxation, anticipation to handle flat, hard serves, and a knowledge of service spins for control in returning slices and twists. The lefthanded slice or the righthanded American twist will bounce, then move toward your left. The sooner you take slice or twist, the less effective they will be; therefore you stand in as much as possible for spin serves. The later you take flat, hard serves, the less the forward pace on them;

therefore you want to take them from behind the base line, particularly on a fast court. And so you stay on your toes in anticipation of moving forward for slices and twists or of jumping backward for flat cannonballs.

Strategy during rallies

In volley, the first objective, when serving, is to force a weak return from your opponents or to draw them out of position—in either case, you can then volley or smash for the point. If, for example, either opponent is standing on or inside his base line, volley deep, directly at him and as near to his feet as possible, so as to force a comparatively weak return which you can kill. Or, if you volley deep to the centre of their base line, you will draw at least one, possibly both, of your opponents to the centre, which may give you an opportunity to volley to a corner for an ace. Or you may volley deep to one corner, drawing your opponents apart, and then volley or smash between them through the opening you have made.

The sharply angled cross-court volley to the alley is often effective for an ace, but if it fails, you will probably give your opponents a setup. The extra width of the doubles court and your position to the side of the half-court line provide wide angels and frequent chances to kill a ball by a short, sharp, wide volley; you should, however, volley to kill. The stop volley is often effective, especially on grass courts. Somewhat similar tactics apply to the smash as to the volley. Eventually, you may learn to kill a lob from almost any part of the court; but for the beginner a good general rule is to smash for a kill when you are near your base line. Do not let lobs drop, however, no matter how deep they may be, or you will lose the net position. If the lobbers run in, smash at their feet; if they stay back, smash deep; and in either case, get back into a volleying position quickly. Your partner should tell you if your opponents are following in their lobs; he should also watch the lob and should call if it is going out.

Actually, an important matter about which you must have a definite understanding with your partner is the taking of lobs. Many points are lost on this score, not because the lobs are untakable—but because the partners muddle one another. Here again, so long as you understand each other, you can adopt what method you like, but as a general rule it is easier for the partner standing at the net to retrieve the deep lobs, when the server is running in. It is obviously easier to get off the mark quickly from a stationary position than to have to stop, turn, and retrace your steps. In fact it is almost impossible for the server, if he or she is concentration on getting right up to the net as quickly as possible, to cope with the deep lobs that go over either head, and pitch within an inch of the base line. On the other hand, the player at the net has only to watch the receiver's racket carefully to anticipate the lob, and will then have plenty of time to take the necessary action. Here is another important reason why the server should maintain a strict rule with regard to following up the service. The partner at the net must know what the server's movements are going to be if he or she is to deal satisfactorily with the lobs. If the server is coming in, the net player must not poach—but must be ready to fly back and retrieve the lobs.

When both partners are up at the net, they will of course each retrieve their own lobs. During a rally if one has to run back, the other should move back as well, so as to be on a level. There are fewer "gaps" in the court when the partners are in line with one another.

Your reply to the deep lob (one that you cannot kill) must depend on the movements of your opponents. If they follow their lob up to the net—as they should—then your only chance is to send back a lob, high and deep, one that they cannot reach to smash and which gives you the opportunity of reaching the net position again. If, however, the opponents do not advance to the net when they have lobbed over your heads, then a good-length drive will give you a chance of reaching the net once more. But always remember that when either you or your partner has to lob, if it is not a good one, it will be "killed," and your best chance of picking up a "kill" is by taking up your position outside the base line.

With regard to the short lob which can be smashed, each player should be responsible for those in his or her court, and be responsible for those in his or her court, and those in the centre should be dealt with by the partner in the left court, because they fall on the forehand—whereas they are on the backhand of the right court player, and therefore almost impossible to "kill."

A short, low cross-cut drive should always be attempted if your opponents are slow in regaining the net after smashing one of your deep lobs. If this squeeze play is well executed and followed in without the slightest hesitation, you can steal the net from the servers. It is demoralizing for your opponents to have the net taken away from them in this manner, and you only need to bring it off a few times in one game to break through their service and win a commanding lead in the set. This is, of course, a risky play; unless your drive is low, you will lose the point. But it is so all-important for your team to capture the net, and chances of winning the point from the back court are so much against you that it pays to take chances—not by driving blindly with all your strength, but by finesse.

The lob comes into its own in doubles and can occasionally turn defence into attack if it is not abused. An effective attack sometimes is to alternate deep lobs and short drive when possible. Persistent lobbing sometimes will break down all but the strongest attack. If one of your opponents is not too strong on smashing, you can sometimes steal the net by lobbing deep, preferably to his backhand, and following in. If your opponent lets your lob drop near his base line, take the net.

Poaching is often sound strategy in doubles. When you are serving, for example, your partner, from his net position, can often get a possible volley shot on a ball returned to your side of court, and in such a case, he should take it. Partners who have played together for a long time almost know instinctively when each will poach on the other, but it is a good idea to call out or signal a poach whenever possible. Too much poaching, however, may ruin the game—as well as leave one side of the court open for the opponents to drive over a winning point. A good rule to follow is to poach only when you can execute a decisive stroke.

While shots down the centre usually belong to the partner on whose forehand they come, there should be a prearranged understanding about this and certain other types of shots. In a quick encounter at the net, the partner who has just played the ball generally continues to finish the point if possible. He is warmed up and in close contact with the exchange. However, when this is the case the player not handling the shot or shots must move swiftly to cover any section of the court exposed by his partner's action.

In doubles, when all the players are volleying, many balls are taken which if left alone would go out. There is so little time for your partner to judge the pace and elevation of the ball that he or she has to volley, but you are in a better position and should call "out" clearly and distinctly. Again, if there is nay doubt in your mind as to which of you is going to rake a certain ball, a quick "yours" or "mine" will prevent you from hampering one another.

Doubles tips

The game of doubles is much more than serve, return of serve, and volley. It is a game of skill, tactics, and headwork. Here are suggestions for good doubles:

1. The partner who is winning his serve more easily should start serving first in each set.
2. Lefties should serve on the sunny side since it is *not* the sunny side for them.
3. Lefties are generally better in the right court since it gives them an opportunity to poach off the forehand.
4. When in doubt, hit down the centre.

5. Do not baby setups; hit them!
6. Lob frequently; drop-volley rarely; drop-shot never.
7. Vary your returns of serve and disguise them.
8. If you never poach, your opponents need be less careful about their returns.
9. Never be angry with a partner who is passed when he poaches.
10. Do not moan or look unhappy when your partner misses.
11. When you have pulled the opponent wide to the backhand court, you and your partner should cover your forehand alley and the centre, leaving your backhand alley open. The reverse holds true on a wide ball to the forehand court.
12. Play the weaker opponent and play his weakness.
13. Practice the doubles shots you do not know—except in a match.
14. When a lob goes over your head and your partner goes back for it, cross over quickly so that you are not both caught on the same side.
15. Show good manners: do not call shots on your opponent's side (unless asked), do not quick-serve, do not stall, and do not blame your partner if you lose.

Mixed doubles

Mixed doubles is a branch of the game which calls for some principles very different from those used in either singles or men's doubles. The same methods of play that are used in other doubles do not often hold good and frequently cannot be brought into use because of the inequality of the two partners in this kind of a game. That is, the principle of the weaker link of a chain applies very strongly here, and it is very difficult to prevent the opposing players from selecting the woman on your side of the net for attack and by directing their strokes to her, to reduce the opposing strength to the level of the weaker player's game. To prevent this only one way seems practicable, and that is to get the woman up to the net at the first opportunity and then to direct your strokes, if you be the man partner, so as to support her in that position where she can be of the most value to her team.

The woman is usually more valuable to her side at the net the man at the back of her court, unless he can work his way in and support his partner in the volleying position, when both might hold the attack safely together. The difficulty is in getting the woman up to the net safely. When her man partner serves, there is no question but that her place is at the net, and she can take up her place is at the net, and she can play. Similarly, when he is the receiver, she can take the same position safely and he can support her by his first return.

But when the woman serves and when she is the receiver, the man's place generally is at the middle of the base line to cover any return that the other side can make. For the dangerous run that the woman must make toward the net without being caught halfway up with the ball at her feet, a strategic stroke must be made that will give her the needed time, and this is not always afforded by the return of the adversaries. If both of the opponents are back in their court, perhaps the safest way to secure the desired position is to drive deep into the woman's corner on the other side and have your partner run up behind this drive.

If the other woman is on the same side of the court as your partner, this can be done at the first opening, but if they are diagonally opposite, it is always safer to have her cross over to the side opposite her woman opponent, and then make the run to the net on the first deep drive into the woman's corner. If the woman on the other side is playing at the net, this chance is not open, and the next alternative is to lob deep over the woman's head and your partner can then run in under this lob at all. However that may be, one of these two devices should be used and manoeuvred for until your partner can reach the net safely, after which anew situation presents itself.

With the woman at the net, this tactical position is usually sound, and if the other woman has also reached the net, then it is a matter of better tennis on even terms or better strategy that ought of win. With the woman against you at the base line and your partner at the net, the odds are all in your favour, of course, so long as you can prevent the opposing woman from running in. Unless she be exceptionally clever at passing, a deep drive into her corner ought to let you follow it up safely, and with both yourself and your partner at the net together, victory is almost certain with the ball kept on the woman's side of the court, and about even if the opposing man gets a chance at the play.

With both women in the volleying position, the play between the two men generally is diagonally across the court, and it should be aim of the clever player to keep his drives well over in front of his partner, so that from her position she will be able to cover as much territory as possible. To play to the other corner leaves the "open diagonal" of the court wide open and limits the partner's usefulness to covering a very small sector of the court. When the opponent follows the same tactics and simply tries to outdrive you, a splendid variation is to work him far out to the outside of his court to meet a diagonal drive and then to lob deep and low over his partner's head and follow the play up to the net. The effect of this play is to bring the man on the other side directly behind his partner, leaving them doubled up and the other side of the court entirely unguarded.

If you follow this play up to the net quickly, the court will be wide open for a kill and nothing but a lob or a brilliant passing stroke will save the other side from losing. The greatest danger of this play is that the man opponent will be able to cross quickly enough to smash, but if the lob is low and well placed to the side of the court, thè will find it very difficult to get there in time, especially if he was far over to the other side before.

When volleying with all four at the net it is in most cases best to aim at the woman, for she is likely to be not only less strong in the wrist for the return, but less able to keep up a series of short crisp shots. She may volley finely, but she has not the endurance of the man. Do not think, however, that she will be slower at chasing lobs or less reliable when dealing with them. She will not be so punishing overhead, but she will be as well, possibly better, able to deal with them after the bounce, and swifter to reach a good position for that purpose. There are many other variations of play for mixed doubles, but success in this game depends largely on getting your woman partner up to the net, and keeping her there safely so her position covers as much of the court as possible. Naturally, the woman who volleys well is much the stronger partner, and to select one who volleys badly is to court defeat.

The service is a big advantage in mixed doubles, and the man should always serve first as he ought to win his own service game 70 percent of the time with evenly matched teams. The struggle usually develops around the winning of the games in which the women serve and both of the men are expected to win their own service games.

4

THE GAME

Before you could hold a racquet and hit a ball you played Hand Toss Tennis and learned to score and count a game. Next, you learned the grips and swing mechanics for the forehand and back-hand and you now have a workable, if imperfect, circular serve. You now have the three key strokes it takes to play tennis. Now comes the fun part. Find an opponent and put your three stroke game to work in the crucible of competition!

Opponents. Finding an opponent can be more difficult than learning to play. Begin at home, line up family members for practice sessions or playing games and sets.

At all times try to arrange to practice and play with opponents of your skill level or better. Remember, however, that you were a beginner once and if a less skilled player asks you for a game be gracious-accept.

Reviewing the Game. The game consists of four points. The first point is "fifteen," the second point is "thirty," the third point is "forty," and the fourth point is "game." There is no such call as "five!" The serve is initiated from the right court to begin the game and when the total number of points played is an even number. In like manner, when the number of points played is an even number. In like manner, when the number of points is an odd number, serves are made from the left court. The right is commonly called the "deuce court" and the left court is called the "add court." Games are terminated by serves coming from the left court except when the score is 40—15 or 15—40. In such an instance, the game may be terminated by a serve from the right court.

SERVING RULES AND COURTESIES

Players should observe the following rules and courtesies when serving.

Serve position. The singles service position should be taken behind the baseline and about a foot and a half from the centre marker. The doubles service position should be taken behind the baseline and midway between the centre marker and the doubles sideline. In both positions, the server stands to the right of the centre marker when serving to the right service court and to the left of the centre marker when serving to the left court. These positions are not inflexible but are highly recommended since they position the server properly for subsequent play action in both singles and doubles. Remember: The first serve begins in the right court. All practice serves must be taken before play begins.

Service faults—foot faults. Rule 8 of the official USTA rules states that a server throughout the delivery of the serve shall not change position by walking or running and not touch, with either foot, any area other than that behind the baseline within the imaginary tension of the centre mark and the sidelines. A foot fault on the first service is a "fault" and loss of serve.

A foot fault on the second serve is a "double fault" and a loss of a point. Foot faults are a needless and wasteful practice for the server and take totally unfair advantage of the opponent. Begin right, practice serving without foot faulting!

Balls served into the net or that fail to land in the correct service court are called "faults." The receiver should call "fault" on the first serve and "double fault" on the second serve.

A service "let" is a replay of either the first or second serve. The two common lets are: ball hit net cord and goes into proper court; interference during delivery of the serve over which the player(s) have no control. Example: A ball rolls onto the court from an adjacent court during delivery of the serve.

Serving courtesies. When serving, there are a number of general courtesies to observe.

— Before serving the first point of the first game, hold the balls up to indicate that the game is about to begin.

— The server must wait until the receiver is ready before serving either the first or second serve. If the server isn't sure the receiver is ready, ask "Are you ready?"

— The server is responsible, in a unofficiated match; to call the game score out loud before each turn of service. Always call the server's point first.

— Return all balls to the server after the point is over and preferably when the server is looking!

— Let service faults go by. Do not hit them back idly

and wildly thus interrupting the rhythm of the serve or play on other courts.

— Call service faults quickly, clearly, and decisively. If unsure, play the serve as "good."

The rally. During a ground stroke rally balls must land inside the outer boundary of the playing court or on the line of the outer boundary. In singles, the outer boundary lines are the singles sidelines and the baseline. In doubles, the outer boundary lines are the doubles sidelines, which include the alleys, and the baselines.

Line balls are good! This also includes serves which strike the service line, centre service line, and that portion of the singles sideline which bounds the proper service court.

Call "out" or signal by pointing to indicate that a rallied ball lands outside the proper boundary lines.

Interference during a rally, over which players have no control, requires that a "let" be called and the point replayed.

Balls must be allowed to land outside the boundary lines to be called "out." Catching a wild ball that is obviously going out is illegal. In such cases the point goes to the striker. In like manner, a ball that hits the body or racquet of a player before striking the court surface is loss of point for the player who was struck.

RACQUET READY—PLAY

Armed with the foregoing procedures, courtesies, and rules, follow A and B as they play C and D one complete game of tennis. Except for the order of service when playing more than one game, this sample game serves to illustate the procedures for both singles and doubles play.

A—B VS. C—D

Players C and D win the spin and elect to serve first.

1. D stands behind the baseline about midway between the centre mark and the doubles sideline to begin play for the first point. D holds up the two balls to indicate that the side is ready and play begins. The first serve is a fault. The second serve is good and player B hits the ball cross-court and out. The score is 15-love.

2. D serves from the left side, first serve is good, players rally the ball back and forth, C hits the ball into the net. The score is 15-all.

3. D serves from the right court. The first serve is a fault, second serve is a fault. Receiver calls out "double fault." The score is 15—30.

4. D serves from the left court. D hits a good hard first serve. A hits it quickly and too hard and the ball flies over the baseline. D signals the ball is out by pointing and calling "out!" The score is 30-all.

5. D serves next from the right court. The first serve is good and players rally back and forth. B hits a low drive over the net and between C and D for a winner. The score is 30—40.

6. D serves from the left court. During the ensuing rally A hits the ball into the net. The score is now tied three points each or "deuce." Players must win two consecutive points to win the game.

7. D serves from the right court or "deuce" court. The first serve strikes the net cord but luckily falls into the correct service court. The receiver calls out "let first serve." D reserves the first serve into the net. Receiver calls out "fault." The second serve is good and players rally until C moves downcourt to hit the ball in midair (volley) for a clean put-away shot. The score is "advantage server."

8. D serves from the left or "add" court. The first serve is a "fault." The second serve is good but a ball from an adjacent court rolls into the service court just as receiver attempts to return the serve. The receiver calls "let second serve." D re-serves the second serve which is good. A spirited rally ensues, D moves downcourt and hits the ball in midair (volley) for a winner. C and D win the game!

Playing reminders

1. The server is responsible for keeping score. The server's point is always called first. The server, therefore, should call the score out loud before playing the next point. Any misunderstanding or errors can be easily corrected between points.

2. If confused about where the next serve is to be delivered, remember that an odd total of points played means a left court serve and an even number of points played means a right court serve.

3. Players are responsible for calling "faults" on the serve and "out" during a rally. Hand signals help make these calls quickly visible. Players often have their backs to opponents when calling or noise in the area makes it difficult to hear the call. Pointing

a finger signals "out." Holding the palm of the hand down as in baseball signals the ball was "good".

4. When the score becomes deuce, the server should announce the score by saying "advantage server" or "advantage receiver." A common call is "add out" for receiver's advantage and "add in" for server's advantage.

This sample game covers practically all of the situations the beginning player encounters in the game situation. Let's review what was covered. The serving order was right, left, right, left, as is proper. Checking that a total of three points had been played (item 4) assured the correctness of the left court serve at 15-30. The score became deuce (item 6) and players experienced playing advantage points. Both kinds of "let" situations occurred" one in which the ball hit the net cord and the other from outside interference. Proper language was used in calling the score, lets, and loss of point. Players used their three stroke game and in addition moved down court to hit a short ball in midair, therefore, they experienced in play a stroke yet to be learned.

Playing "games" is fun and each game played introduces the player to a variety of additional needs. Game rallies are not like setting the ball up to oneself or getting a good rebound off the wall. Game rallies can be deep, short, hard, soft, and from severe angels. Remember, your opponent is not there to give you a good comfortable shot to return as you did in self-toss tennis or practice against the wall. The opponent's objective is to hit the ball into open spaces on the court and at angles so that you cannot return it. Playing games introduces you to a variety of shots and the need to learn more than the three strokes already acquired. Playing practice games is fun and instructive, however, after a point it is time to package these games into the official way of determining a winner in tennis, namely, by playing sets that become matches.

SET AND MATCH

A regulation set consists of six games won by one player. The winner must be at lest two games ahead of the opponent in order to win the set. A common winning set score may be: 6—4; 7—5; 8—6; 9—7; etc. A match consists of playing the best two of three sets. Most recreational, club, and regional competition is determined by a best two of three set match. However, professional tennis and national championships for men are generally three of five set matches. Women, juniors, and senior players adhere to the two of three set matches. Package your name play into sets and matches and extend your playing experience and begin to learn how to be a winner!

Playing a set like playing a game requires a player to learn certain procedures, courtesies, and rules. The following are some of the rules and procedures players need to observe.

— Players must change sides after each odd total of games. Changes occur after game 1, 3, 5, 76, etc. On change-overs players have a ninety second rest period for towelling off, adjusting equipment, or quenching their thirst.

— If the set ends in an even total of games, players must not change until the completion of the first game of the net set. Example: Set ends 6-4, players stay and play one game, then change sides after game 1 of the second set.

— If the set ends in an odd total of games, players change, play one game, and change again. Example: 6-3, players change sides, play one game, and change again.

— In doubles play, players must maintain their chosen sides for receiving for the entire set. Should the left court receiver wish to play the right court the change can be made at the beginning of the second set but not during a set. In like manner, the service order in doubles must be maintained for a complete set. Any change in service order between partners must be made at the beginning of the second set.

If the set is tied at six games all, players may choose to play a "tiebreak." The official United States Tennis Association tiebreak is the "Seven of Twelve Point Tiebreak." In friendly matches, players may choose to play a tiebreaker or to simply keep playing until one player or one side has a two game advantage. In tournament play, however, to play or not to play a tiebreaker and when to play it, i.e., each set or just the final set is determined by the tournament committee. For recreational play it is a good idea to play a tiebreaker as often as possible in order to be thoroughly familiar with the procedure. To learn the procedure, when not play best tow of three tiebreakers with an opponent to "practice" procedures and experience the psychological impact of playing the tiebreak as opposed to playing a game. Assuming that you are at 6 games all in a set, let's play a 7 of 12 point tiebreak.

TIEBREAK TIME

The winner of the tiebreak is the player in singles or the side in doubles that reaches seven points first with a two-point advantage. Points in the tiebreak are counted 1, 2, 3, 4, etc. Scores may be 7—0, 7—4, 7—5. The service order, i.e., who serves, is the same as in the set. The player who serves first in the tiebreak gets only one turn of service which is made from the right court. After the first turn of service, each turn of service by all other players consists of two turns, i.e., left court and right court. Note that all service turns after the first will begin in the left court. To check which court the serve comes from, simply add the score and if the total score is odd it is a left court serve. If the score is even it is a right court serve. Example: Odd point totals are 1—2; 3—2, etc. Even point totals are 2—2, 4—2, etc. Players change sides when six points have been played. Example: 3—3; 4—2; 5—1. Should the score in the tiebreak become tied at 6 points all, play must continue until one player has a two point advantage. In this case the tiebreak may end in a score of 8—6; 9—7; 10—8; etc. Remember to change sides at 6 points all and every six points after that juncture. The tiebreak counts as one game of the set and is recorded as 7—6 with the actual score of the tiebreak in parentheses as beside or slightly above the set score of 7—6. A recent ruling by the United States Tennis Association allows the actual score in the tiebreak to be recorded as a single digit since the winning points are constant.

Tiebreak reminders

1. In the tiebreak, winning your turn of service is very important! Emphasis, therefore, must fall on getting

the first serve in as often as possible. A high first serve percentage means a better chance to win the tiebreak.

2. Because of the frequent change of service turns in the tiebreak, it is vital for the server to announce the score before serving to prevent mistakes. Remember: Odd point totals mean a left court serve, even totals mean a right court serve.
3. In doubles if a player serves out of turn, the following should be observed: If the error is discovered after the first point has been played and before the next point is played, the order of serve should be corrected immediately. If discovered after the game has been played, the order should stand as altered. All points played and faults incurred shall be counted.

Tiebreak practice

Although the tiebreak is a fact of life in modern tennis, it is quite possible for players to play a lot of tennis and never be in a tiebreak situation. This is especially true of beginning players and players who do not play in an organized league or club situation. Players, therefore, may be knowledgeable about the tiebreak but because of the infrequency of play they become rusty and forget just how it goes. In view of this, it is a good idea for players in general and beginners, especially, to play the tiebreak as a mini-game during practice sessions to keep in touch with the procedures and scoring.

TENNIS ETIQUETTE

Knowing and observing some of the customs and traditions of the sport will make you more comfortable and secure in your relationship with the friend you play regularly or the opponent you play occasionally. Unfortunately the majority of tennis competition of all types is played without officials. The players, therefore, have the responsibility for making decisions. Many of these decisions are guided by custom, tradition, and unwritten rules. Yes, you must know the rules but, as importantly, know the customs, traditions, and unwritten rules that apply to player interaction before, during, and after play.

Before play begins, custom and tradition include being on time for the match, greeting and chatting in a friendly manner with your opponent, offering and deciding who furnishes the balls for play, and spinning the racquet to decide serve, receive, or side. Whether your opponent is someone you play with regularly or infrequently it is best to do all of the friendly talk and banter before going on court. Talking during warm-up and play is frowned upon, therefore, all news, gossip, and laughs should be exchanged before play.

Ideally, a player should warm up before meeting the opponent for the match. This would allow the prematch warm-up to be conducted satisfactorily to both players within the customary time limit. Remember, the warm-up is not a practice session! During the warm-up, courtesy dictates that you hit balls to your opponent and that you not return practice serves. In friendly social play players may agree on the length of the warm-up period. In such cases the length would depend on total amount of time each player had allotted for play on that particular occasion.

During play, talking is customary and allowable on occasions when the server calls the score before serving, receiver calls a fault or let, players call lines or compliment each other on a "good shot." Making unnecessary noise during the play of a point is taboo. An occasional self-admonition to "run" when trying hard for a shot is acceptable. Refrain from loud "postmortems" after a point or during the exchange of sides between games. Displays of temper, use of vile language, throwing your racquet, or slamming the balls around after losing a point spoil and disrupt the game for your opponent and those playing on adjacent courts. If you are losing or playing poorly, don't cast a dark cloud over the match by sulking and stalling. Instead, make position comments about your opponent's play and move from point to point and game to game at a normal pace. Remember, play must be continuous.

Making calls and decisions quickly and firmly during play avoids delaying the game and creating unfriendly feelings. Players are responsible for all calls on their side of the net. If you are in a poor position to make a line call, you may ask your opponent's opinion but never ask a spectator! "I don't know" and "I didn't see it" calls are not reasons for playing a let. They are, instead, occasions for quickly and graciously awarding the point to the opponent.

The "benefit of the doubt" type decisions constitute the oldest tradition in tennis. They include: ball touching player before bouncing; player touching net during play; contacting ball before it comes over the net; double hit, carry, and double bounce. The players involved in these infractions are best qualified to make these decisions and it is a customary expectation that players make the call on themselves quickly and firmly.

Two thorny decisions that players must deal with are: Did you hear the let? Was the receiver ready? In the case of "hearing" the service let, either player in singles may make the call. In doubles, players nearer the net are more likely to hear and call the let. It is customary for the receiver to make the sole determination as to readiness for the serve. The receiver, therefore, must not attempt to return the serve in order to preserve this right. The server should look at the receiver and try to determine if, indeed, the receiver is ready. Should this fail and the receiver appears to be indulging in acts of "gamesmanship" the server should simply ask "Are you ready?" The latter is annoying and distracting but effective.

In multicourt complexes, balls rolling onto courts are a constant problem. Both etiquette and rules apply, depending upon the circumstances. Balls rolling across your court during play provides a basis for a let. Balls rolling from your court onto another court demand that you wait until the point in progress is finished before asking politely "ball, thank you." To avoid aimless return of a stray ball, hold up your hand so the player returning the ball will know to whom the ball should be returned. It is extremely rude to continually return an obviously faulty first serve. Returns of this kind not only ricochet around your court but too often needlessly interfere with play on other courts. Be courteous, allow all obvious faulted first serves to go by an trap in the fence behind you. It is courteous and efficient play to catch faulted second serves and return them to the server when the server is ready to collect balls for the next serve.

An opponent who foot faults badly or at all on the

serve is committing a fault. The rule covering the foot fault regulates the most decisive stroke in the game and should be observed. The receiver in singles and the receiver and partner in doubles can legally call foot faults in nonofficiated matches but only after all efforts and appeals to the server have failed.

What is the score? To eliminate arguments resulting from forgetting or getting mixed up in keeping score, the server should call the game score before serving each point. In like manner, to keep the set score straight, the server should call the set score before the first service of each game. Should an argument ensue and an agreement cannot be reached, begin play at the score upon which both sides or players agree. Should this fail, spin a racquet.

Final tips! Dress neatly and appropriately; do not embarrass your friends or opponents by showing up in jeans, jams, or jogging shoes. Carry an extra racquet. A broken racquet or string can spoil the fun for you and your opponents. Call well ahead of time when you need to cancel a playing date. Help secure a fourth if you cannot be the fourth player in doubles. In tournament play, notify tournament officials if you must default and save your opponent a needless trip. Last but not least, don't withdraw from a tournament just because your opponent is a better player. Be a tiger; meet the challenge and profit by playing up.

Each match has its beginning and ending. Regardless of the final results, the conclusion of the match should be friendly and courteous as the beginning. Players in doubles should first shake hands with their opponents. Friendly banter and positive comments are in order. In social play, often a "next time". To play is agreed upon. Players should retrieve all loose balls on their side of the net and give them either to the owner, if the match was a social event, or to the winner, if the match was a round of tournament play. It is customary in singles to leave the court with your opponent. In doubles, players customarily all leave together, if they do not, be sure to wait and walk off with your partner. An after-match get together for friendly postmortems and refreshing libations is the sign of good fun, good friendships, and good tennis.

5

PLAYING STRATEGY

Now that you've earned your wings it is time to not only play tennis but play more tennis! Armed with basic strokes, rules, and courtesies you are ready to challenge all within your ability level. The more play you experience the more you will understand the need for learning the strategies that go along with singles and doubles play.

Receiving position. Stand at the junction of the baseline and singles sideline; stand behind the baseline for first or hard serves and inside it for second or short serves. This is the receiving position for singles and doubles. This position bisects the two possible wide angles open to the server. It gives the receiver a 50-50 chance at either the wide outside angle to the forehand or the inside angle near the junction of the centre service line and the service line or "T" to the backhand. This position is not inflexible but is recommended as a basic "home" position until strokes and strategy covering all the "what if the serve does, etc.," can be developed.

Returning the serve. The return of serve is the second most important stroke in the game. The return of serve is the receiver's opportunity to force a "service break" and thus it becomes an offensive weapon. The return of serve should be practised as much, if not more, than the serve. The return of serve should not be treated as just another ground stroke. Ground strokes should be adjusted to make reliable and consistent returns of serve.

Returning techniques. The receiver must learn to actually "see" the ball as it contacts the server's racquet in order to "read" the flight path before the ball crosses the net. The ability to move quickly depends upon the "see the read" technique. A second important aspect of returning service is foot action. In preparing to receive keep "nervous feet!" The weight should be on the balls of the feet. Hop just as the server tosses the ball. Nervous moving feet plus the hop is the springboard action needed to move forward and on to the oncoming serve.

A third technique of great importance to a good return of service is the swing action. Two keys to an effective swing or stroking action are (a) to turn the shoulders, and (b) use a short straight backswing. For the second serve, move inside the baseline closer to the service line and repeat the shoulder turn and short backswing action. Except in the early stages of learning, most serves are too quick to allow for full backswings. For fast serves "chip and charge" is better than executing "full lovely ground strokes".

Targets for return of serve. In singles there are three primary targets, return deep and down-the-line off the forehand to opponent's backhand; return deep and cross-court; return low and down the middle. In order of importance, the return must be deep; return to the opponent's weakness; and return low and down the middle to reduce angles and cause the opponent to hit up. Beginners should return balls high over the net to achieve the depth need. Balls returned four to five feet over the net will land deep because of height rather then strength applied. High cross-court returns give beginners time to position themselves for the next shot. In doubles, there are two "bread and butter" returns for beginners: cross-court short returns into the alley and crosscourt deep returns to the server's position. The more experienced player adds a low down the middle return and the offensive lob over the net player's head. Remember: The most important thing about a return of serve is that it goes back over the net and stays in play. Skill in returning serves is not necessarily the byproduct of good ground strokes. Be sure to practice return of serves along with other strokes equally.

Singles. The two most important strategies for the beginner are keeping the ball in play and hitting the ball deep. Keeping the ball in play puts pressure on your opponent to "do something" to win the point. Concentrate on keeping the ball in play to give your opponent ever-increasing opportunities to "do something" which more often than not results in an error.

Beginners achieve depth by hitting the ball high, four or five feet, over the net rather than applying power or strength to the shot. Hitting deep high balls that land near the baseline offers two advantages, it gives the hitter time to get into position for the next return and it reduces the return angle and the aggressiveness of the opponent.

A third strategy consists of hitting into open areas on the court to make your opponent move. This should be employed as soon as you begin to control the direction of your returns. Keeping the ball in play, hitting deep to the baseline, and moving your opponent combine to give you your first offensive and aggressive strategy. Moving your opponent from side to side and up and back creates an opening into which you can hit a clean winner or, at least, cause a weak return. Moving and hitting keeps the opponent from getting set to hit with power and control.

The cross-court return is especially useful in developing these strategies. First, it is a safe return since it passes over the low point of the net at the centre. Second, the side to side diagonal angle gives five to six feet more hitting space or target area. And finally, the angle of the cross-court shot moves the opponent off court and away from the centre thus making it difficult to return to position for the next shot.

Doubles. The ultimate strategy in doubles must wait on the development of the serve and the acquisition of a full complement of strokes. However, beginners can play and enjoy doubles using the three stroke game. The following strategies are sound fundamentals upon which to build an enjoyable doubles game

Receiver: The receiver should concentrate on keeping the return away from the net player. The standard returns to make are cross-court deep to the server's position an cross-court short into the alley. The cross-court deep return opens the court on the server's side for play away from the net player. The short cross-court return moves the server off court and out of position leaving an open court between the opposing players.

Receiver's partner: The partner of the receiver should stand just inside the service line and four of five feet from the centre service line. From this position, the receiver's partner can help call service faults and, once the ball is in play, move up to within six to eight feet of the net. This position offers the receiving side a chance to experience an occasional volley, thus learning by doing.

Server: The beginner's serve is not strong enough to allow for the usual "serve and volley" technique in doubles. Therefore, the server must wait for a short ball to have an opportunity to move downcourt. Once downcourt the server should stay along the service line to protect against lobs. This position gives the serving side two players who may experience hitting an occasional volley or even an overhead. Serves should be directed at the receiver's weak side to hopefully cause errors or weak returns. Remember, avoid hitting to the net player!

Server's partner: The server's partner or net player stands just inside the singles sideline and about six to eight feet from the net. From this close-to-the-net position, the net player can cut off returns by volleying them firmly deep or at angles into the receiver's court. The net player should also volley any returns that pass over the net between the centre strap and the alley. This means moving along the net to pick off volleys or errant shots. Should the opponents lob over the net player's head, partners should switch sides, i.e., the net player moves fully to the other half of the court at the net while the server moves in like manner to the opposite half of the back court to return the lob. Players should remain in switched positions until the point is over, or play demands a second switching of sides.

Polishing your game

Your game play so far should have alerted you to the fact that a three stroke game of serve, forehand, and backhand does not meet all the stroke needs a full court game of tennis requires. Playing has taught you that there are really two games: one played from the baseline and one played in the forecourt. Let's complete your stroke arsenal so that your game can become offensive and aggressive. To do this we will begin with the volley.

The volley

The volley is a stroke used to intercept the ball in midair before it bounces. It is an attacking weapon and is used to finish off points quickly and decisively. This action returns the ball to the opponent more quickly and with greater possible angles. Volleys may be hit from any place on the court but most often they are hit from the forecourt, i.e., between the net and the service line. In singles, the volley turns a defensive baseline game into an offensive, aggressive, and attacking game. In doubles, the volley is of even more importance. Doubles is, in fact, a volley game with baseline trimmings!

Volley grips. The Eastern forehand and backhand grip used in hitting the ground strokes is an already learned grip and, therefore, may be used in the initial learning stages. Changing from the forehand to the backhand grip when volleying poses a problem. Since the volley is played in the forecourt the ball comes to the hitter over a shorter distance allowing little time for elaborate grip changes. The Continental grip proves to be a more useful grip in that one gripping hold can be used for forehand, backhand, and overhead volleys. In the Continental grip the V formed by the thumb and index finger should be on the flat top late of the racquet handle. This position is a slight turn left from the Eastern forehand grip. A continental grip gives a flat racquet face position for hitting on the forehand side and a slightly open face position for hitting on the backhand side. Its chief charm is in requiring no change of grip when volleying. Try it-you will like it.

Shoulder high volley

Forehand. Begin in ready position, racquet up opposite eye level and elbows forward of rib cage. Rotate shoulders to the right, move toward net with the left foot, extend arm and racquet from the elbow with a sharp, crisp, punching motion to contact the ball out in front between the right shoulder and the net. Racquet head should follow through out and over the vision tape line of the net. Weight ends on left foot. Point the racquet in the direction of the flight and bounce of the ball. Practice cues: "Turn shoulders, step, punch, and point." Practice moving toward the oncoming ball with small steps rather than one big lunge or step. Small steps keep the feet underneath the body and allow the player to "move to and through" the point of contact. The moving body weight adds a feeling of power and strength to the "punch and point" extension of the arm.

Backhand. Begin in ready position, racquet up opposite eye level, and elbows forward of rib cage. Keep a light hold on the throat of the racquet with the left hand. Rotate shoulders to the left pulling the racquet head back with the left hand holding the throat, move toward the net with right foot, extend arm and racquet from the elbow with a quick sweeping motion. Contact the ball between the left shoulder and the net out in front of the left shoulder. Racquet head follows through and the top edge of the racquet points out over the net in the direction of the flight of the ball. The follow-through should end higher than the vision tape on the net. Practice cues: "Turn shoulder, sweep, and point!" Practice emphasizing the uncoiling of the shoulders from left to right as the arm sweeps the racquet head out to contact the ball and follow through out over the net. Coiling and uncoiling the shoulders gives good strength to the sweeping motion in the backhand volley. Keep the wrist slightly cocked throughout the execution of the backhand volley. Practice moving to the ball with small steps as in the forehand volley to keep body weight a part of stroking. Do not lunge with one big step! Instead, move smoothly to and through the ball.

The following three Sport Experiences are a sequence of steps for learning the volley. The catch and throw practice will make it easy for players who play or watch baseball to understand the similarities. The choke-up volley will help players with weak hitting skills to learn good ball contact and the importance of letting the racquet do the work. Finally, the alternate volley practice holding the racquet at full length makes practice "gamelike" and the movements like those needed in game play.

Choke-up volley

After practising the "catch and throw" volley action on both forehand and backhand, try making ball and racquet contact by using a "choke hold" on the racquet. Hold the racquet at the throat to shorten the leverage. Move to the ball on the forehand side and rebound it off the strings. Repeat by moving to the ball on the backhand side and rebounding the ball off the strings. The racquet in this choked gripping position is in effect a large extension of the palm of your hand. On the forehand, strike the ball with the racquet or extended palm of your hand. On the backhand, strike the ball with the racquet or extended back of the palm of your hand.

Full volley practice

Now you are ready to hold the racquet at full length. Use a Continental grip and practice alternate volleys, i.e., move to and through the forehand volley, resume ready position, and move to and through the backhand volley. Working or practising at the six to eight foot distance from the net should produce many successfully volleys over the net. After working at this distance, move back halfway between the service line and the net and repeat the alternate volley practice. Finally, begin on the service line, move in halfway to hit the forehand volley, then up to the six-foot distance to put away the back-hand volley. Repeat this last practice beginning with a back-hand volley and finishing the sequence with a put-away forehand volley.

Overhead smash

The net player in doubles and players in the volley position in singles often get to hit "set-ups." A set-up is a ball that is the result of a weak offensive lob or errant ground stroke or "moon ball" that passes over the net player's head in easy reach. The mechanics for hitting the overhead volley are the same as for the upper half of the circular serve and should be used instead of trying to hit a high backhand volley or a high forehand volley. Overhead volleys in the forecourt should be hit with this overhand volley motion.

Begin in ready position, turn shoulder to the right as the right arm and racquet move up and over the head, right elbow points to the "sky," racquet head is down behind the head and upper back. Move with small steps or slides until left shoulder is under the drop of the ball. Throw the racquet head up and out at the ball, racquet head follows through out over the net. The finish should be higher than the net and point in direction of flight of the ball.

Practice cues: "Ball up, racquet up, touch back, move under ball, throw and contact, follow through." Ball should be contacted at the highest point of the arm and racquet reach, weight transfers from right to left side. Pointing the left finger up at the ball helps visually check whether the ball is over the left shoulder in a comfortable hitting position. A good shoulder turn allows the shoulders to coil and uncoil for greater hitting power.

Overhead smash practice

Stand between the net and service line with left side turned to the net. Hold the racquet in hitting position, elbow pointing to sky, racquet head down behind right shoulder. With the free hand toss a ball as high up as possible between the service line and the net. Let the ball bounce, move under the bounce, and punch the ball out and over the net.

Low volleys

A low volley is a ball contacted below the vision tape on the net and sent up and over the net with a low trajectory. Low volleys require good touch and good racquet string contact to get solid rebounding from the centre of the racquet. In the forehand volley, turn the shoulders to the right and extend the arm and racquet out at a 45-degree angle and down pointing the top edge of the racquet at the base of the net. This opens the racquet face for good ball contact. Move toward the net contacting the ball forward off the left foot, follow through up and out over the net level. the technique for the backhand low volley is the same except the shoulders turn to the left, racquet is extended out and down to bottom of net with racquet face open. Move to the ball and contact out opposite right foot, follow through up and out over the net level. Again, move with small steps instead of lunging with one big single step. Practice on both sides to learn to keep the ball low over the net and to get good short angle, from both sides.

Low volleys

The hitter stands six to eight feet from the net or a racquet's distance and one step from the net. The partner stands opposite the hitter at the junction of the centre service line and the service line. The partner underhand tosses low trajectory balls across the net at a 45-degree angle to the hitter. The hitter moves in and rebounds balls by contacting them below the net level. Practice directing the balls cross-court and down the line. Work on both the forehand and backhand equally. The hitter may work alone by tossing the balls with the left hand. Step and contact the ball below the vision tape level. When working alone the hitter will have to let the ball bounce, then hit it over at an angle. This is not, of course, a volley but it will give the contact and angle practice used when actually volleying the balls low too high.

Lob mechanics

Swing the racquet back, head low and face open, step forward contacting the ball below waist level, and follow through out and net high. Let the racquet strings rebound the ball up. The flight of the offensive lob should be a flat arc. The flight of the defensive lob should be sharply up and deep. For the forehand lob, step left to contact the ball below waist level. For the backhand lob, step right to contact the ball below the waist level. In most cases, players are stretching to get to the defensive lob. The offensive lob is a deliberately made shot off the ground stroke that allows easy execution.

Offensive lob

Station a partner six to eight feet from the net at the centre of the court. Partner underhand tosses the ball to the forehand side of the hitter stationed behind centre mark and baseline. The tossing partner then quickly extends the racquet arm's length overhead. The hitter sets up an offensive lob over the tosser's extended racquet. Tossing partner" jumps and reaches" to check clearance of the lob. A good offensive lob will clear the jumping reach of the net tossing partner and land well inside the backcourt area. Repeat on the backhand side.

Defensive lob

Station a partner across the net on the service line.

Partner underhand tosses the ball over the net to the forehand side of the hitter. The hitter is stationed at the centre behind the baseline. The hitter hits a defensive lob over the net and high over the head of the partner in the opposite court. To be good, the ball should land deep inside the baseline. Repeat toss to backhand side.

Rally and lob

Players (singles) rally ground strokes from the baselines. Count out loud each time the ball is hit. On an even count one player is designated to move into the service line and allow the opponent to defensively lob overhead. Repeat rally and count. On an odd count the other player moves in to the service line and allows the defensive lob to be hit overhead. Players are assigned to be the "odd" or "even" player. Play ten turns to see which player has the highest "lob in" count out of ten. As a rule of thumb, nine out of ten defensive lobs go "out!" With this in mind take defensive lob practice seriously.

Serve and lob

Partner serves a medium speed deep serve and moves into a volley position inside the service line. The receiver sets up an offensive lob. If the lob is good it will clear the jump reach of the server and the receiver gets one point. If the server misses the put-away the receiver gets the point. Repeat working from both right and left courts. Server should serve four times, two balls allowed as in a gamelike situation. First player to a total of ten points wins.

Short serves and second serves

Short serves are rather common in the early stages of learning to play tennis. Short second serves are fairly common in play at all stages. In either or both cases the short serve deserves special attention. Short serves are in effect an approach shot and the receiver should take advantage of it by (a) adjusting the receiving position inside the baseline thus closer to the service line, and (b) learn to attack the serve by moving to and hitting through the return. This action can produce an outright winner. Make it a habit to adjust your receiving position for the shorter second serve. Study your opponent's serve and learn to adjust your receiving position to accommodate either serve.

Returning short serves

Work against a player who is learning to serve to get maximum practice against short nonpaced balls. Practice cross-court and down-the-line returns. Work with a target area marked with ball containers, towels, ball pyramids, etc. The target for cross-court shots should be about two feet in from the junction of the baseline and the single sideline. The target for short cross-court angles should be at the junction of the service line and the singles sideline. These targets set up on both sides of the court will do for the down-the-line shots as well. Practice both the forehand and backhand returns. Variation: Return the serve and move into volley position and hit two volleys. the server will hit one serve and set up a forehand and a backhand volley. Repeat this variation for all returns in both right and left service courts.

Target practice

Work with a partner who has a highly consistent serve. Practice returning serves without rallying out the point, i.e., serve, return serve, and repeat. Use a visible target such as empty ball containers, hula-hoops, or four ball pyramids. Set the target for deep down-the-line shots off of the forehand and backhand; deep cross-court shots off of the forehand and backhand; short cross-court shots off of the forehand and backhand; and short and low down the centre shots off of the forehand and backhand. It is important to work against a variety of servers. After working against a highly consistent serve, work against one who spins the serve and one who puts pace or power on the serve. If these characteristics can be found in one server so much the better.

Serving consistency

The object is to serve the ball over the net and into the proper service court. Assume the singles service position for the right (deuce) court, serve two balls. Assume the singles service position for the left (add) court, serve two balls. Continue alternating serves, two to the right court and two to the left court in "gamelike" fashion. Score 100 percent if both serves land in the service court. Score 50 percent if only one serve lands in the service court. Four turns of 100 percent serves is excellent consistency. Four turns of 50 percent is fair consistency. For turns of 100, 50, and zero percent show a need to work on your serve consistency. Be sure to repeat serve consistency practice from the double service position. Variation: Serve only one ball to each service court instead of the usual two. This will check the consistency and percentage of "first serves in."

Players who are having difficulty in executing the full circular serve may try the consistency Sport Experience with the "half serve."

Placement practice

Make a four ball pyramid by placing three balls on the court surface and one on top of the three. Place one four ball pyramid a foot in from the service line and a foot in from the single sideline in the left and right corners of the right and left service court. Assume the singles service position and serve two balls at the target in the outside or left corner of the right service court. Repeat by serving two balls at the target in the inside or right corner of the right service court. Continue alternating practice in the right and left service courts. Scoring: 100 points for a knockdown on the first serve of the four serves allowed in each court; 75 points for a knockdown on the second serve; 50 points for a knockdown on the third serve; and, 25 points for a knockdown on the fourth serve. Repeat scoring procedure beginning at 100 points when practising the four ball serves to the left court.

Ball machine practice

Practising against a ball machine allows multiple practice on the forehand and/or backhand to one target at a time. Set the machine for service to the forehand in the right court and practice multiple returns of serve cross-court then down-the-line. Similar setting can give multiple practice on the backhand from the right court. Repeat, work from the left court.

Spinning the ball

Learning to make the tennis ball move on its several axes or spinning the ball adds finesse to your game. Learning to spin is one side of the coin; the other is learning to return a ball to which spin has been applied. Therefore, it is important to understand the action of the spins used in tennis. The three types are topspin, slice, and sidespin. the topspin and slice are the most common.

Topspin. The spin is in the direction of the flight of the ball. this action is generated by starting the racquet below the ball with a flat or slightly closed face and moving up through the ball to a high finish in front and to the opposite side of the body. The results are a higher flight over the net with a sharp drop to the surface followed by a quick forward and upward bounce.

Slice. The spin is in the opposite direction to the flight of the ball. This action is generated by starting the racquet higher than the ball with an open face racquet and moving down and through the ball to finish out and over the net. This high-low action causes the ball to rise or float, lose forward speed, and produces a low bounce depending upon the playing surface. On hard surfaces the ball may bounce straight up and away from the approaching hitter. On slow surfaces the ball will "die" or hug the surface.

Sidespin. The ball is made to spin on its vertical axis by hitting across the back of the ball from right to left or reverse. The action makes the ball "curve" in the direction of its spin. Sidespin finds limited use among players but is effective to achieve severe slicing action on the serve.

Applying spin

Once you have established good fundamental stroke mechanics you have an easy reference point from which to apply topspin and slice action. Your ground stroke swing up to this point has been a relatively flat motion. the racquet moves forward parallel to the surface and contact is with a vertical face. With this action as a reference point, adding spin involves simply contacting the ball on the upswing or on the downswing. Applying spin to the ball comes more naturally on some strokes, therefore, try these first.

Slice backhand drive and volley. In both strokes the racquet head begins high in the backswing and there is no grip change. To impart spin, simply swing the racquet to the ball keeping the racquet face open at contact and in the follow-through. This high to low motion causes the racquet head to pass down and through the ball left to right to impart the backspin. Be sure to make a good weight transfer to the right foot to assist in applying forward motion to the stroke to achieve depth.

Topspin forehand. The swing is low to high. The racquet begins below the ball with the face slightly closed, or it may be vertical, and swings up to and through the ball finishing in front and to the opposite side of the body. Modest topspin action is generated without changing the grip. To develop greater topspin, however, change to the Western grip in which the V is on the flat back of the racquet handle. This a one-eighth turn to the right from the Eastern forehand grip.

Topspin serve. The toss should be made back toward the right shoulder to allow the racquet movement is like "brushing" the strings across the ball. The Continental grip gives a modest angle to the racquet face, however, for greater angle use the Eastern backhand grip.

Slice serve. The serving action is between the flat serve and the topspin serve. The toss is to the right side of the body so the racquet passes around the outside of the ball. The Continental grip gives a modest angle. The Eastern backhand grip gives a greater angle.

Topspin backhand. The two handed backhand is ideally suited to producing topspin. The low to high action is natural and the ball can be hit with greater force and still stay in bounds.

Practicing spin serves

Before trying either the topspin or slice serve, try bouncing a ball off the edge of the racquet frame. First use a Continental grip and practice the "hammer and nail" action of bouncing the ball from the edge of the racquet. Next, try the same action using the backhand grip. Then try serving keeping in mind the idea of hitting the ball on the edge of the frame as you swing up to contact the ball. This should assist you in getting familiar with the angle at which the racquet "brushes" up through the ball.

The one handed backhand will require work and patience. The swing action requires a full shoulder turn with racquet head low opposite the left knee. The forward swing is a sharp upward motion taking the racquet face from below the ball through and up over the top. The Continental grip allows a vertical face at contact, thus the need to "roll the wrist" at impact. the Eastern backhand allows a closed face at contact, thus less rolling wrist action. The follow-through is high and to the opposite side of the body.

Slice forehand. The swing motion is from high to low. The racquet head begins up with a well-cocked wrist. the racquet face is open so that in the high to low swing the racquet strings pass down and across the ball from right to left finishing with an open face racquet in the follow-through. Weight transfer is important to impart forward thrust to the ball.

Singles and doubles strategy

Singles may be defined as a baseline game with net trimmings. This definition, however, is somewhat tempered by the type of court surface being played upon. Hard surfaces are more conducive to the serve and volley type game whereas slower surfaces foster the baseline game.

Singles play in the early stages of learning is typically a baseline-type game with occasional chances to move into the volley position. Once you begin to polish your game by adding strokes and learning to spin the ball, your singles play will become more aggressive and offensive.

Doubles may be defined as a net game with baseline trimmings. Net play is the essence of good doubles. The serve and volley and the volley and overhead are the key strokes needed to make your doubles the exciting game it is by its very nature. In the early stages of learning of more advanced strokes. Enjoy playing and as strokes are added strategies can be employed. Doubles is a team game and the teamwork and camaraderie it engenders makes it a popular way to play tennis.

Volley opportunities in singles

Possibly the most common way to get into a volley position in singles is by moving in on short shots. this is referred to as "making an approach shot." The approach shot may be hit down-the-line or cross-court.

The object is to move the opponent off court and court and cause a weak return which can be easily volleyed into the open court.

A player should be able to move into a net position under a first serve in singles if the serve is to the outside and deep so that it moves the receiver off court. In such a case, the server should follow the line of the serve into a volley position and return the volley to the open court. The serve and volley under the second serve is a gamble, at best, and should be tried only as a surprise move. The best chance, therefore, is to move into the volley position under the first serve and/or play along the baseline until a short shot or other opportunity presents itself for getting into a volley position.

A forcing shot is the third opportunity to advance into the volley position in singles. A forcing shot is a shot that moves the opponent off the court to one side or which causes the opponent to hit on the run. Forcing shots result from down-the-line or cross-court shots. In either case they make the opponent move over back of the alley or actually outside the doubles sideline to make a return.

The fourth means of taking advantage of the net area is to hit to the opponent's weakness. After a few games players should know what side, forehand or backhand, gives the opponent the most trouble. Deliberately playing to the weakness of the opponent will provide openings to gain a volley position and put away weak returns for quick and easy points.

One of the smartest strategies for gaining the net advantage in singles is to set up a high defensive lob which lands near the baseline. This forces the opponent to move back near the fence. While the opponent is manoeuvring into position and looking up at the ball, move quietly down court into a volley position and surprise the opponent by hitting a quick angled "cut off" volley for a winner!

Volley opportunities in doubles

The primary job of the net player in doubles is to volley. The net player's position should be six to eight feet from the net just inside the singles sideline. This position gives room for the serve to be delivered and allows the net player to move or poach along the net in his or her half of the court. The net player will get forehand and backhand volleys and will be able to step back for short overhead volleys resulting from weak lobs and high errant ground strokes.

The server in doubles should serve and move into a volley position on or inside the service line after each serve, i.e., the first and the second serves. Thus the serving team has two players in position to volley on each half of the court. In doubles, players learn to "close in" to the net when the ball is opposite them in the opponent's court. This means that the player who close in is opposite the ball and the hitter. When player A closes in, player B would shift diagonally back and toward the centre service line to close the middle and be in a position to switch behind the partner for an offensive lob from the opponents.

The receiver in doubles should move into a volley position after hitting a weak or short serve cross-court or low and deep to the feet of the oncoming server. The receiver should also move in under a cross-court return if the server fails to serve and volley. A third possibility for the receiver is to move into a volley position after hitting an offensive lob which causes the opponents to switch sides. These actions put the receiving team in volley position before the serving side has a chance to get into volley position.

Bonus stroke—the lob

The lob is almost a forgotten since the mechanics are basically like the forehand and backhand ground strokes. The similarity often leads players to think it is an easy shot so why practice? The lob requires touch and control, therefore, it should be practised often. The lob has specific and strategic uses which should be understood.

There are two distinct lobs, the offensive lob and the defensive lob. The offensive lob should be hit just over the "jump reach" of the net player and land well inside the baseline. The arc and drop of the ball prevents the net player from running around and back to make a return. More often the server or partner of the net player has to switch over to pick it up. The offensive lob is a definite offensive weapon in doubles. It is also effective in singles particularly against an opponent who continually plays tight or close to the net. It is disastrous against a player who runs to the net instead of moving into a volley position.

The defensive lob is used to recover court position after having been forced out of court along the baseline. The defensive lob is hit the high ball flight gives the hitter a comfortable chance to recover good court position.

6

TENNIS DRILLS

There are thousands of tennis drills. Some coaches and players adamantly recommend certain drills, whereas others advocate different ones just as strongly. How can coaches judge what tennis drills are best? In the last 10 years researches have extensively investigated the effects of different types of practice drills on the learning of motor skills. This research has produced two very interesting finding that can help coaches make wise selections. One of these discoveries is that how well a skill is learned is greatly affected by the extent to which performers must vary their practice performance. For example, players who wish to develop a good forehand ground stroke could spend a large part of practice drills fielding moderately paced, waist-high balls. And all the balls could be hit, for example, to the same crosscourt target so that players would not have to make big stroke adjustments. Researchers call this a low variability type of practice because players do not have to significantly vary their shots. On the other hand, players could attempt to develop good forehand ground strokes by organizing drills that require them to make rather extensive adjustments in their shots. In a high-bouncing shots. On the other hand, players could attempt to develop good forehand ground strokes by organizing drills that require them to make rather extensive adjustments in their shots. In a high variability form of stroke, players must play low-and high-bouncing shots and hit balls both down the line and at short angles.

Which of the two approaches is the more effective? Based on research, high-variability practice appears much superior. The research suggests that players who practice a wide variety of fore-hand ground strokes would be much better at hitting high- and low bouncing balls and more able to accurately hit down-the-line and short-angle shots. Also, such players would be able to adjust to types of forehand ground strokes that have not been practised. They would even be able to hit waist-high crosscourts as well as (or better than) players who spent most practice time drilling only on waist-high crosscourt shots.

The other finding regarding practice drills is that the sequence in which a performer practices different motor skills, or variations of a motor skill, pronouncedly affects the quality of learning. One possible order of practising different shots is to hit several overheads, then some volleys, then some ground strokes. This is called blocked sequencing because all shots of one type are chunked together in a switch from one shot to another-an overhead, then a volley, then a ground stroke, and so on. This method of practice is called *mixed or randomized* sequencing.

Players practising only serves can also choose between blocking practice trials or mixing them up. They could hit only flat serves first, then only spin serves, which would be blocking. Or they could practice flat and spin serves in mixed or random order, frequently switching between the two.

Motor-learning research strongly supports randomized sequencing practice trials that require players to frequently switch from one skill (or skill version) to another. Although players have been found to perform better during practice when they are allowed to block their trials, this type of practice does not well prepare them to handle game-like situations, which usually call for a highly random order of shots.

Practice variability

Practice variability research indicates that the more variable the practice experiences, the better players learn to make needed adjustments in motor skills. Because tennis demands constant adjustments, it follows that coaches minimize the time allotted to drills that do not require much response variability. Wise coaches design drills and manipulate environmental conditions to demand a variety of stroking adjustments.

Drills designed to *groove* a swing are typically the ones that elicit relatively low response variability. A grooving drill has a player standing in one place on the court repeatedly hitting the same shoulder-high volleys to the same spot under the same environmental conditions. The popularity of such drills is due in part to the fact that players perform them well. Consequently, players (And some coaches) believe that such drills are the best way to learn. Players and coaches who defend these kinds of drills use terms like consistently and *automatically* in reference to making the shot. "I can refine this shot," they say, "to the point of never missing it," and "If can handle this easy shot, the more difficult ones will take care of themselves."

But will they? This kind of reasoning might sound good, but research simply does not support it. The results of many studies clearly suggest that spending a lot of time on low variability practice does not best prepare a player for a match. Repeatedly hitting the same shoulder-high volley will not prepare the player to cope with low volley, balls that stretch or jam the player, balls that approach rapidly; or balls that. And importantly, repeatedly hitting the standard shoulder-high volley is not even the best way to learn to make shoulder-high volleys.

The argument applies to all drills that require minimal stroke variation. These drills are not *bad* for a player's game, but they are not nearly as effective as drills that demand a diversity of swings. Prudent coaches take a close look at all their drills and make sure that most of them do not fall into the grooving category. In their place, they develop drills that foster greater practice variability. Now let's consider some high-variability drills and how they can be coordinated with environmental settings to promote a better practice session.

Drilling with a partner

When team-mates are drilling together they should intentionally hit shots that require a wide spectrum of responses from each other. This is true regardless of the stroke they are primarily practising. Two example drills will illustrate how to maximize shot-making variability. Once we have shown how to vary partner volleying and overhead practice, you will readily see how to apply similar techniques for other shots.

A volley drill begins with a feeder and a container

of balls. The feeder is instructed to hit shots require all types of volleys. The feeds should include soft and hard shots, topspin and backspin, low and high balls, and shots both down the line and crosscourt. the volleyer adds further variety to the drill by moving around, so that some of the shots are hit from no-man's land, others from just inside the service line, and others from very near the net. The volleyer should also attempt to vary the direction of his or her shots so that some are crosscourt, some down the line and some are stop volleys. The speeds of the volleys should vary as well. A partner drill for overhead smashes starts with a feeder dropping and hitting lobs of divers trajectories. The lobs should range from extremely high ones to those on the borderline of being high volley. Similarly, some lobs should be deep and others short. Some should be directed over the backhand side and others should require a rapid shift to the forehand side.

Meanwhile, the smasher's job is to mix spinning defensive returns with forceful kills. The returns should be attempted cross-court, up the middle, and down the line. Another means of maximizing variability is for the smasher to begin the drill from different positions. An initial position virtually on top of the net will force the player to field shots while moving back. A deep starting position will require forward movement and a different kind of over-head execution.

These two example drills differ from most partner drills commonly used by coaches in one fundamental way. In these drills the players do not attempt to hit the ball back and forth to each other. It is fair to say that most traditional partner drills emphasize keeping the ball in play, which usually means players will have long rallies with low shot variation. In these drills, variety is not planned and happens only by accident. The players seldom have to perform unorthodox movements. They do not have to adjust their swings to nearly the degree that playing a match requires. In some drills players are not even expected to attempt the more difficult shots when they present themselves. IT is as if they are coached to work hard at the shots within their immediate range and not worry about the unusual ones-which is hardly what occurs during a match.

Rallying drills have their place. They are appropriate during warm-ups and can be important part of everyday practice drills. Sometimes you simply may not have the court space or adequate ball to implement the high-variability drills. Besides, keeping a ball in play has an exciting, challenging element. IT can be great fun, it permits the concentration of many shots in a limited time period, and players derive satisfaction from the evidence of skill improvement in the form of longer rallies. Coaches are rightfully reluctant to cause players to miss out on this kind of morale-boosting experience.

Perhaps we can clarify our partner drill recommendations by outlining four specific suggestions.

1. Have a preseason talk with your players about how practice variability can improve their games. Your coaching prestige will be enhanced when you show them you have invested the time and effort to learn how skills are best learned and have developed some practice plans to help them. When players are

aware of the potential benefits, they will enthusiastically work at new variability practice drills both during and outside of practice.

2. Incorporate some high-variability drills into most of your practice. The examples posed earlier should guide you in your planning.
3. Continue to use rallying drills. Although these drills may not provide highly variable experiences, they offer other benefits. Having both types of drills in your playbook will enable you to change drills frequently, which helps avoid motivational problems associated with stale practice sessions.
4. Use compromise drill versions of the above types of drills. For instance, use rallying drills in which the players consistently hit shots right to each other and only occasionally throw in a zinger. The zinger does not have to be an attempt at an all-out winner, just a shot a bit harder or wider than normal. In such a drill the challenge might be in attempting to get the ball back under control.

There may be a need to address those coaches who find high-variability partner drills or compromise versions unacceptable. You love rallying drills and are reluctant to instigate anything that might terminate rallies sooner than necessary. We urge you to at least consider discouraging your players from always assuming the exact same rallying positions. Do not always allow volleyers to belly up to the net: demand that sometimes they volley from deeper in the court. Encourage your ground strokers to sometimes play their shots from inside the baseline and sometimes from well behind the baseline. These kinds of slight changes can painlessly be added to your drills and will interject some valuable variety.

Another painless procedure is to frequently rotate rallying partners. Different players hit different kinds of strokes and demand different response adjustments. Keep one caution in mind when rotating partners. Although rotation is desirable, some degree of skill-level matching should be maintained. A mismatch in partner skill will likely result in less variability for stronger players. Weaker players will either not be able to return shots or will hit shots poor in diversity (they might not have the ability to hit hard shots with various spins). Such situations cheat the more talented or more experienced players of opportunities to learn to handle different shots. Also, in mismatch situations the better players sometimes feel obliged to limit their shot variety to avoid overwhelming the weaker player.

Drilling and the environment

In our discussions to this point we have considered two basic ways of increasing the variability of players swings. One way was to change the flight characteristics of balls hit to the players by varying speeds, spins, and directions. The other way was to have players hit balls with different speeds, to different targets, and from different court positions. One environmental factor is the wind. Hitting into the wind as opposed to with the wind causes a diversity of responses. Whereas hitting into the wind requires big, forceful swings, playing with the wind calls for shorter, more controlled shots.

Although no studies have been done on the effects of practising in windy conditions practice variability research would strongly support players doing so.

Stroking adjustments demanded by a strong wind prepare players to compete under such conditions-and with spring schedules, wind-blown matches are more the rule than the exception. Coaches probably err in assuming that because player performance suffers in the wind they should move practice inside or postpone it. Adverse conditions that require major stroke adaptations are probably ideal learning experiences.

Playing in the wind is one way of taking advantage of the environment to change the swings of your players. Other ways are playing on different surfaces, playing with different types of rackets. Because changing environmental influences are valuable learning experiences, coaches should expose their players to them.

This is not to suggest that coaches subject their players to such controllable environmental variables immediately before or during a match. Assuredly athletes need to become accustomed to the balls, the playing surface, and so on. But usually one day's practice or less is sufficient to readjust to playing circumstances. Players with a limited range of experiences need to practice adjusting to various circumstances and to changes in the environment. Many young players fall in love with a favourite kind of racket and marry it. Or they develop an early aversion to playing either indoors or outdoors and avoid doing so with a passion. Some players will not stoop to playing with balls more than an hour old. Coaches surely recognize the types.

The time will come when these people must compete under unfamiliar conditions. Tournaments will be moved inside, racket strings or frames will break, balls will not be promptly replaced when they become light or *fuzzy*. Even if players miraculously avoid such unexpected occurrences, variable practice experiences produced by environmental factors still make sense. The variety improves players overall ability to make the shot variations that will be required if them.

The world's finest players are highly competent on all types of surfaces and in all kinds of wind conditions. Granted, the Navratilovas and Lendls play better on a surface suited to their style, but they win on all surfaces. Of course these players have great innate ability, but isn't it conceivable that their varies experiences of playing under all conditions contribute to their greatness?

Take as an example the strong 1984 U.S. Davis Cup team that lost on clay in the finals. Some might suggest that the loss stemmed from Sweden's specialized practice on clay and the lack of specialization by the American team. Motor research fully supports the idea that training drills should be designed to closely approximate game conditions. A we know, clay courts favour a groundstroking style of play, whereas hard courts place a premium on aggressive attacking and volleying. To be successful on clay, players must spend a large part of their practice on that surface.

However, concentrating the majority of practice on the conditions to be encountered in a tournament is one thing-limiting virtually all practice to those conditions is something else. Adherence to the principle of practice variability suggests that players benefit from experiencing conditions dissimilar to those they will most likely encounter. In actual practice, the vast majority of American players grow up almost exclusively on fast courts. Until the time comes when Americans have a significantly larger amount of practice on clay and still lose to those who have specialized more, we have no good reason to believe that variability should not be planned into our practices.

Drilling and the beginner

We have suggested incorporating various procedures and environmental factors that requires players adjustments in their swings. Coaches might assume that practice variability and playing under different conditions is fine for players who already possess excellent swing mechanics and are good enough to handle and learn from these more difficult kinds of drills. But in regard to weaker players, or players revamping a technique, coaches might consider high-variability drills too difficult, thinking the drills might cause the players to become more frustrated and that their techniques could suffer.

Such thoughts are sound and need to be addressed. A beginner (or an old hand revamping a stroke) needs drills that produce response variations. Research shows practice variability is an important ingredient for people just beginning to learn a new skill. Coaches simply cannot afford to ignore this.

Agreed, coaches must be careful not to overwhelm beginners participating in a drill where they are completely unsuccessful and correct form is unattainable. Avoid the problem of undue talk difficulty by systematically variability into practice. For example, assume you and a player have agreed that his or her back-hand drive needs a major change.

Do not have this player engage in the normal procedure of spending lengthy practice sessions standing in one place, receiving consistently paced balls, and trying to return them down the centre of the court. Neither have the player immediately running, hitting severe slices, and trying to spin-angle passing shots. Instead, introduce just one of the elements of variability constant except the height of the ball bounce. The balls could be tossed so that one must be played at shoulder height, the next at knee height, and the next somewhere in between. Then, in another practice session, manipulate the speed of the delivered balls. Ask the player to try different shots, such as soft crosscourts or hard down the lines. Or introduce a moving element into the drill. All these variations should be introduced *singly*. Eventually, you can start altering a couple of variables at a time. Ultimately, the player should have to deal with multiple variables that begin to resemble match environment.

You can see that the idea is systematic progression. Do not over-whelm the player with too much at once, but do immediately begin teaching how to make adjustments. Some coaches have done players a disservice by not progressively introducing them to coping skills. Players who have been trained to hit waist-high, moderately paced ground strokes will have their form break down in competition and consequently become discouraged. Suddenly they are not hitting the shots they thought they had mastered. The swing they developed for the standard shot no longer serves them well. The range of their experience proves to be too limited to allow them to figure out how to generate different shot adjustments. As a result, they are unable to cope.

The primary requirement tennis places on us is the need to adapt shots to a changing array of demands. The strokes of tennis contestants must undergo constant adjustments to balls approaching at different speeds, from different directions. Furthermore, players have to hit those uniquely approaching balls in different directions with various degrees of speed and spin. In short with the possible exception of some serves, no two swings players make in a match can be exactly the same if they are going to succeed. When we keep a player from experiences shot variations, we are only postponing the inevitable. There is no royal road to tennis success. It's better to systematically introduce practice variability from the start. By doing it this way, we facilitate the transition to the real tennis world.

Drilling with the ball machine

Unlike live opponents, ball machines cannot deliver balls in a highly variable way. Although some machines project balls with different speeds and oscillate to vary the direction, the speeds and directional changes they achieve generally vary much less than what players will encounter in matches. Furthermore, ball machines do not produce the dramatic spin variations of match play, an inability that reduces the swing variations required of players. Consider how much players must adjust their groundstroke swings to play low-skidding, sliced drives and high-bouncing topspin shots. Or how much they must adjust their overheads to hit topspin lobs rather than defensive, backspin lobs. Because ball machines call forth relatively low response variability, their effectiveness in teaching players to make stroke adjustments is limited. For that reason, nonmachine drills are better for developing the adaptability skills of players. In most cases, coaches would be better off having people assume the role of the machine. Armed with a basket of balls, coaches, assistants, or team-mates could be trained to efficiently feed balls to a performer in great variation-low skidders, exaggerated topspins, short balls, etc. This variability could be suited to each hitter's unique needs and abilities.

Even partner rallying drills, previously criticized for not producing enough stroking variety, are probably better than ball machines can be an integral part of nearly every practice, and a scheduled check-out plan for off-day and off-season machine use would be beneficial. One advantage to ball machines is that they are available when trained coaches, assistants and team-mates might not be. They are also good to have when you cannot find an evenly matched partner for a particular player.

Another reason for using ball machines is that they are an ideal practice aid for someone beginning to learn a new swing pattern. The machine consistently projects balls with virtually no variability-an ideal learning opportunity for beginning ground strokes. Smashers and volleyers could use for machine in a similar way, introducing an element of variability by attempting to hit both crosscourt and down the line.

Ball machines are also excellent for holding everything constant as they introduce limited variations for beginners. For instance, a setting that keeps everything standard except for a gradual increment in directional variability provides a good learning progression for a beginner. Likewise, shooting balls at different speeds provides a worthwhile beginning drill for all strokes.

Again, machines *by themselves* do not provide enough practice variety to prepare advanced performers for match situations. However, the third good reason for incorporating ball machines in practice is that, when used with ingenuity, they can create a reasonably varied practice experience-varied enough even for the advanced player. Most machines can be set at different intensity levels, a feature permitting application to numerous different types of shots. For example, the volleyer could practice hitting balls that are both rifled and blooped, the smasher could adjust the intensity to produce very high and very low lobs, and so on.

Directional settings should also be periodically regulated to produce more than just forehand and backhand alterations. By using different oscillating selections in conduction with differing machine placement, players are forced to move different distances to hit returns. Although coaches sometimes set machines to create moving ground strokes, they seldom do so for other shots, which is strange considering most of the lobs, smashes, and volleys players must execute in match play will certainly be on the move.

Besides using different machine settings, players can augment swing variety by assuming different court positions to create different return attempts. We have already considered different starting positions and shots to create response variety, but here are some specific suggestions. A player might set up in a doubles net position as though his or her partner were serving. The machine is aimed to simulate down-the-line and crosscourt service returns. The player plays the crosscourt returns as if poaching in a match, waiting as long as possible before moving directs down the line, the player will generally attempt to put the ball away by hitting crosscourt into the gap between envisioned opponents.

One final comment wraps up the discussion of ball machines. Accelerating advance in scientific will continue to affect tennis. We can envision the time when practice variability will be widely recognized as an effective practice strategy and when technology will respond by designing ball machines capable of providing much more variety than today's models. With the push of a button, the machine will deliver an assortment of ball trajectories; another push and it will produce a still wider range. Other buttons will propel balls with different spins. There are already some machines on the market with progressive settings. The extent of these progressions can only expand, based more and more on scientific research data. But until the day machines become this sophisticated, their limitations must be recognized. Coaches will have to use their intellects to get the most variability out of machines.

Sequencing of practice trials

Ball machines of the future will be programmable to deliver balls in a diversity of sequences-three balls to the forehand followed by three to the backhand, and so on. The reason for this is the contention of many experts that the order in which swings are made can profoundly affect how well a skill is learned. We have already seen that players learn motor skills is learned. We have already seen that players learn motor skills best when practice sequences are mixed rather than blocked. Although performance levels in random drills are not as high during practice, these drills are much better at preparing players for game situations.

Why this is true is not entirely clear. Most experts believe the reason is related to the unequal amounts of effort required by the two practice schedules. Because the mixed practice is more intently on the skill required and the results produced, which results i a deeper learning experience than the automatic repetition of one specific skill.

Before applying the concepts we have described to the design of tennis drills, consider some recent related research findings. A few people have begun to wonder if completely mixed practice is the best way to learn motor skills. The documentation that mixed drills are preferable to completely blocked drills does not preclude that some intermediate level of blocking might be effective. Perhaps a player switching strokes every second or third trial would be better than the completely mixed procedure of switching after every trial.

Although few answers to this interesting question are available, current evidence hints that frequent switching (After every two or three attempts of a skill) is as good as and possibly better than switching after every trial. Not surprisingly, a strong confirmation of these new studies is that mixed and partially blocked practice sequences have definite advantages over completely blocked sequences. To prepare for a tennis match it appears that a player should practice drills that are either completely mixed or predominantly mixed. However, this is not the case. It is safe that the vast majority of current tennis drills involve blocked practice for ground strokes, volleys, serves, etc.. Many drills even go beyond the blocking of shot types. Sometimes coaches and players block within strokes, not only mass repeating ground strokes but actually blocking forehands and be hands. Still greater blocking is exchanges going further narrowing the drill to consist of all backhand crosscourts.

Switch strokes

The first specific drill suggestion is that players do more drills where they frequently switch from one completely different type of shot to another. For example, if they are fed balls, they should hit one or two ground strokes, come in and hit a couple of volleys, hit an overhead or two, then retreat a few steps and hit ground strokes again. This sequence should be repeated several times, perhaps varying the feeds to require both forehand and backhand shots. Serve-and-volley drills and drill in which players alternate hitting lobs and ground strokes are other examples of complete switching between shots.

It is not proposed that *all drills* be a mixing of completely different shot types. Good reasons exist for drills wholly devoted to serves, lobs, and so on. One reason is that players sometimes have a dire weakness in their shot repertoire that cries out for concentrated work. IF a player's lobs are weak and important matches loom near, obviously he or she needs to spend time hitting lobs.

Another reason for using blocked drills is that they are highly manageable. When court space is at a premium, one court can accommodate four simultaneously practice, or two volleyers can work with two feeders. Switching from one shot to another necessitates more court movement and creates greater logistical problems.

Switch skills within strokes

The second specific suggestion is that when using drills of one shot type it is best to avoid blocking within skill. Consider a situation where a player needs to concentrate on serving, either because he or she is having particular trouble with serving or because there is only court space to work on that shot. The player should continually switch between flat and spin serves. Serving actions might be staggered by serving and staying back, or serving and starting toward the net. Also, serves to the middle might be combined with wide serves. Instructing your players to visualize match situations as they practice encourages them to frequently change from one kind of serve to another.

Consider one last example, just as there are different kinds of serves, there are different kinds of ground strokes. Coaches are better off using drills in which players frequently switch off among some of these variations rather than frequently lengthy blocks of time on one stroke. Even when a player is weak in a specific area, continual switching is still the best way. For a player with a weak backhand, interspersed forehand shots are going to further improve the player's stronger forehand and make it more of a weapon. And the switching will increase the overall difficulty of the drill, forcing the player to concentrate harder when hitting the backhand.

7

TENNIS COACH

A classic tennis confrontation took place between Martina Navratilova and Steffi Graf in the 1988 Wimbledon final. Trading shot for shot, the women sprinted back and forth in a superb exhibition of movement and form. Spectators, awed by how these two athletes played the game, undoubtedly wondered what it takes two be that good. There is only one answer: It takes a lot of talent, combined with years of practice and great coaching.

Since tennis originated, played coaches, and most recently sport scientists have examined, players aspects of the game, always trying to improve hoe to is played. An area of particular concern has been the teaching of technique. As various methods to teaching technique exist, each thought to optimise student learning it's no wonder that students are sometimes confused as to which method is best. Two questions emerge: Does the perfect technique exist and, if so, how is it best taught?

Before we consider these questions we should note that coaching has recently entered a technological era with innovations ranging from the highest-performance sports equipment ever to unique methods of stress management related to performance. These concepts have burst upon our age from a relatively new body of knowledge called the sport sciences. How can a coach becomes aware of and ultimately employ the principles of sport science? Over a century ago a wealthy golf enthusiast, Sri Ainsley Bridgland, developed one of the first research teams in all of sport, consisting of anatomists, engineers, and physiologists. Their goal was to discover the hidden secrets of the perfect swing. But after much research, the conclusion at which they arrived was that there is no such thing as a perfect swing. They found that a variety of swing techniques could achieve an optimal outcome and that there would probably be several ways to teach the various techniques.

The same is true for tennis: is no perfect or best way to play the game. Many different grips and swing techniques are required to hit shots of different speeds and with different spins. Look at the game's greatest players: Becker consistently strikes the ball hard, but uses spin well; Agassi uses a two-handed backhand; Navratilova rushes the net with abandon; and graf is one of the world's best baseline players. These players play very differently from one another, but they have one thing in common: They all play very well.

Similarly, there are a variety of good ways to teach tennis skills. No single best way exists. For optimal performance, each player must be instructed individually how best to swing the racket. Some players respond well to a sophisticated, scientific approach; others do better with a kinesthetic approach to movement and stroke production. An explanation of torque and how the length and mass of a racket can affect strokes may be most appropriate for one techniques and using psychological cues. With this in mind, let's examine what it takes to be a skilled tennis instructor and coach.

Attributes of a skilled tennis coach

Most good tennis coaches are easy to identify. Many were good players at one. Usually they have interest in the tennis business, good personalities for relating with people, and sound understanding of stroke mechanics, conditioning methods, and strategy. These competent coaches contribute to the game and affect the lives of their students. However, if these coaches neglect to study ways to improve their coaching skills, they may never rise in the ranks to improve their coaching or help the number of players they possibly could.

The skilled coach is literally a student of the game, a high achiever who strives to excel by learning about all the factors involved in competitive tennis. The outstanding teaching professionals is a jack of all trades who tries to be master of all as well.

An ambitious goal, but it is amazing how weakness can be discovered and improved. And there is always room for improvement.

Becoming a complete tennis coach

It is said of any business that there is no substitute for experience. Experience means much more than simply having been a great player. In fact, great players do not always make great coaches. In a recent television interview one of the world's top players was asked what he would charge to give private lessons. Most people probably expected him to quote a healthy fee, but the player admitted he would never try to teach anyone the game. "I would leave that up to the teachers because they spend so much time studying the game," he said. "I really don't know very much about stroke mechanics and things like that."

This player showed a great deal of character in so responding, but he may have short-changed himself by underestimating his coaching potential. He may not know much about how he actually hits the ball, but he knows a great deal about competition-when to hit which shot, how to handle the psychological stress of a match, how to control the tempo, how to handle the opponent's psyching attempts. No professional achieves world-class status without understanding these and other elements of competition. On the other hand, a coach who has never played the game competitively will find it particularly difficult to coach successfully at the world-class level. However, such a coach, if he or she has studied the game and experienced pressures of tournament tennis at some level, should be able to work successfully with skilled players.

No matter how scientific their methods of analysing skiils, all coaches go through a certain amount of trial and error to isolate Which experiences were negative and to be discarded and which were positive and to be remembered, used, and built upon. Through years of working with athletes, they accumulate a vast amount of information about performance.

The science of tennis

All sport research has increased dramatically in the past decade. The East Germans are renowned for their research in swimming, the Soviet Union for its track and field research, and Bulgaria for its focus on weight lifting. Unfortunately, tennis has only recently begun reaping the benefits of research, but there is definitely an increasing involvement of scientists and engineers in the study of out game. Recent research has made a positive contribution to the coaching and playing of tennis by developing better rackets, devising better performance techniques, improving conditions of player, and producing more mentally tough competitors.

However, the expectations of research must be realistic. Research will not produce a single best way to play tennis. But scientific research can determine which instructional methods are most efficient and effective in the teaching of strokes. A baseline player whose matches tend to last more than 3 hours must be well conditioned aerobically, whereas the inveterate serve-and-volley player whose matches finish in less time may need to train differently. Some types of imagery may not benefit a particular athlete, but some form of relaxation training might. Research helps us understand coaching alternatives and in which cases to employ them.

There are problems associated with research, however. First some research adds no useful knowledge. Coaches are not interested in the fact that Boris Becker can serve harder than Jimmy Arias. That knowledge is intuitive. A second problem is that research is often not presented in usable form. Without reasonable interpretation by the sport scientist, some research fails to convey to the coach or player what the findings imply. Even to a world-class player, the information that the ball is only on the racket face for 4 milliseconds is meaningless. The importance of such a statistic is depreciated by trying to fathom that time in a practical sense. However, such information is valuable if interpreted in usable form. The coach could persuade the player that, because the time of contact is so incredibly brief, it is impossible to roll the racket over the ball when trying to hit with a topspin. This helps the player visualize that topspin can only be produced by brushing the back-side of the ball with an upward stroke from a vertical racket face.

From this one example of the significance of proper interpretation and communication among sport scientist, coach, and player, you may wonder if tennis research is really all that helpful.

Many areas of science have played an important role in developing the game of tennis. The fields of engineering, medicine, physiology, physics, psychology, and sociology all provide information that can expand our understanding of tennis. In one book it is not possible to provide a complete treatise of all aspects of science that are relevant to tennis and coaching.

Today's coaches want to learn more about sport science research and its applications to tennis. As we investigate such applications, we must be sure to put research in proper perspective. Research is not easy to conduct; sometimes it takes years to develop a method to study a problem, conduct the proper research protocol, analyse the data, interpret the findings, and relate them to the public, whose reactions range from scoffs to cheers.

The coach's own experience and judgment play the lead role in how he or she interprets and utilizes the findings of a research project. Knowing that research is not the ultimate answer, consider what you can use in coaching and what might be the best application for your athletes. If some findings do not make sense or appear usable, ask questions. If you still do not seen an acceptable application, disregard the findings until something you can use becomes available. Keep research in its proper perspective, and the rest of this book can be extremely valuable to you.

INDEX